Lion, Giraffe, Monkey, Elephant , Crocodile ...!

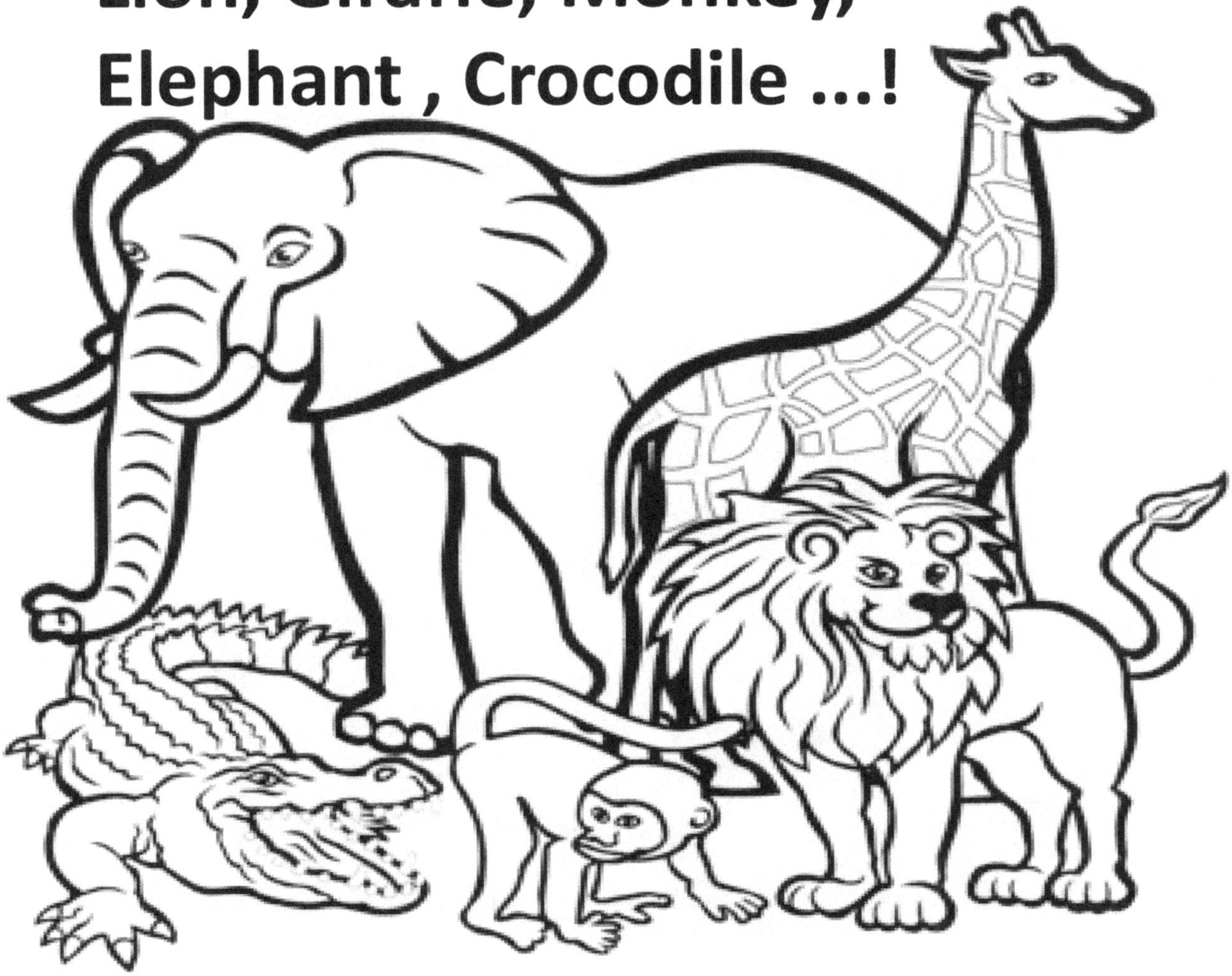

ANIMAL

COLORING BOOK

FOR KIDS

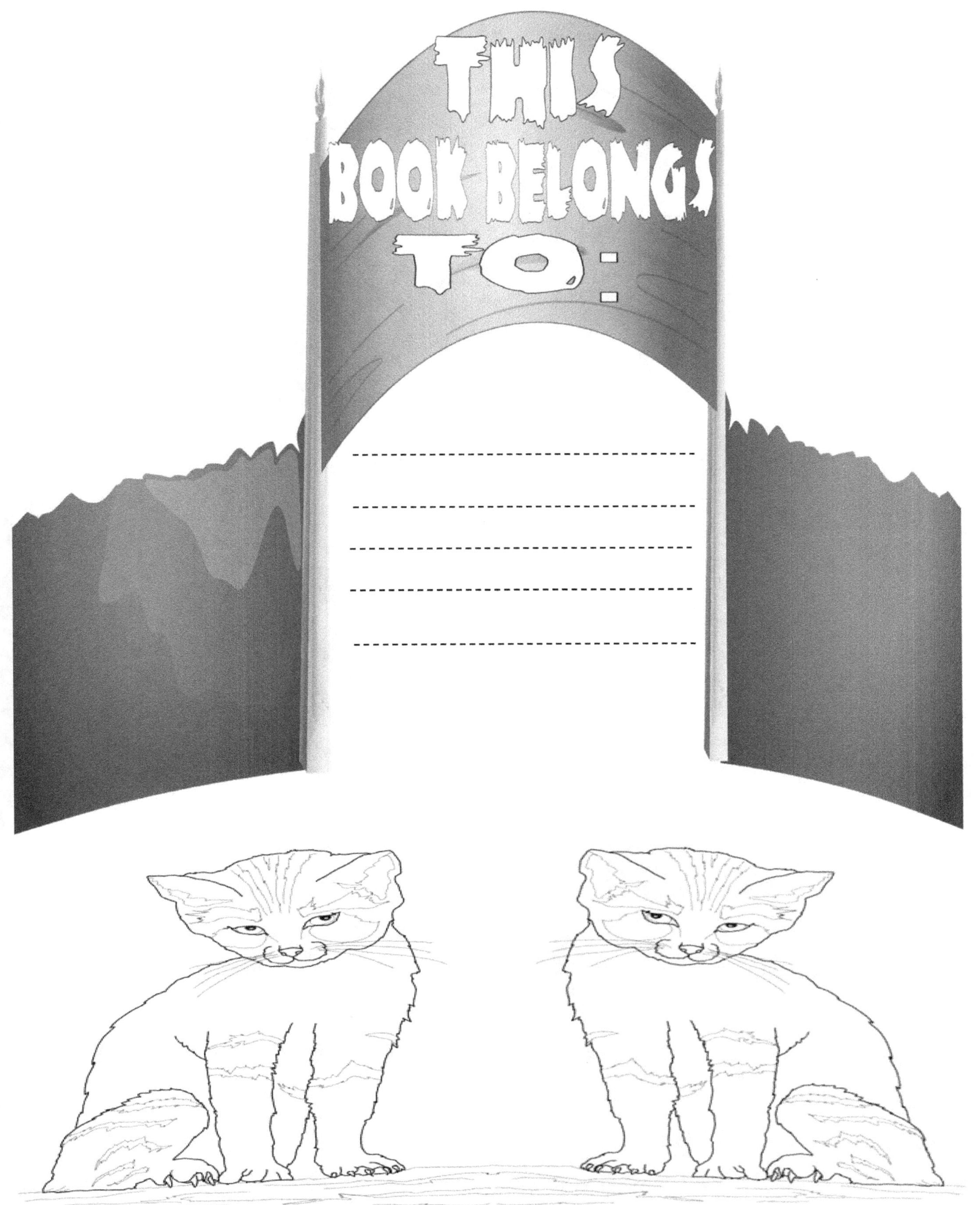

THIS
BOOK BELONGS
TO:

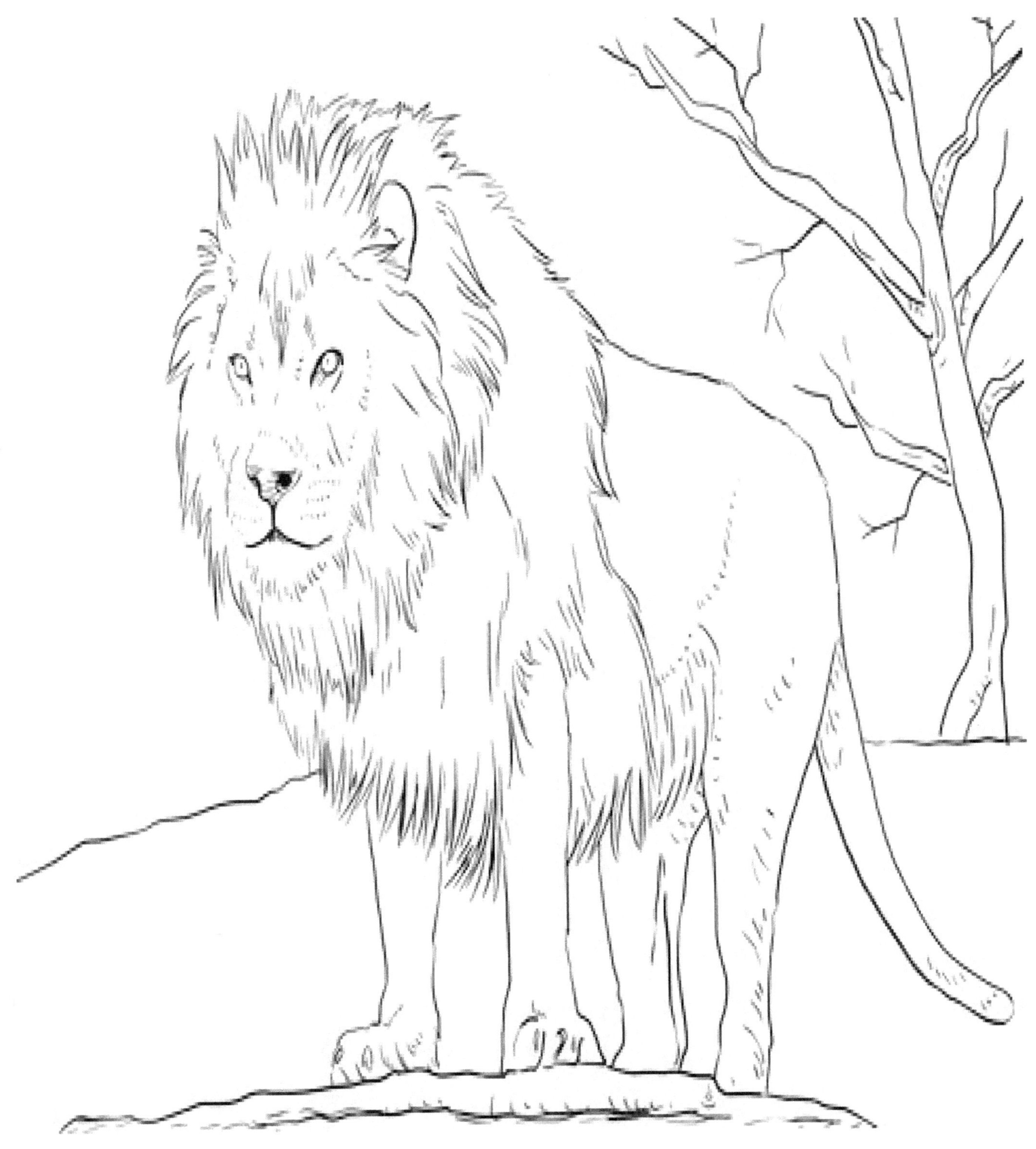

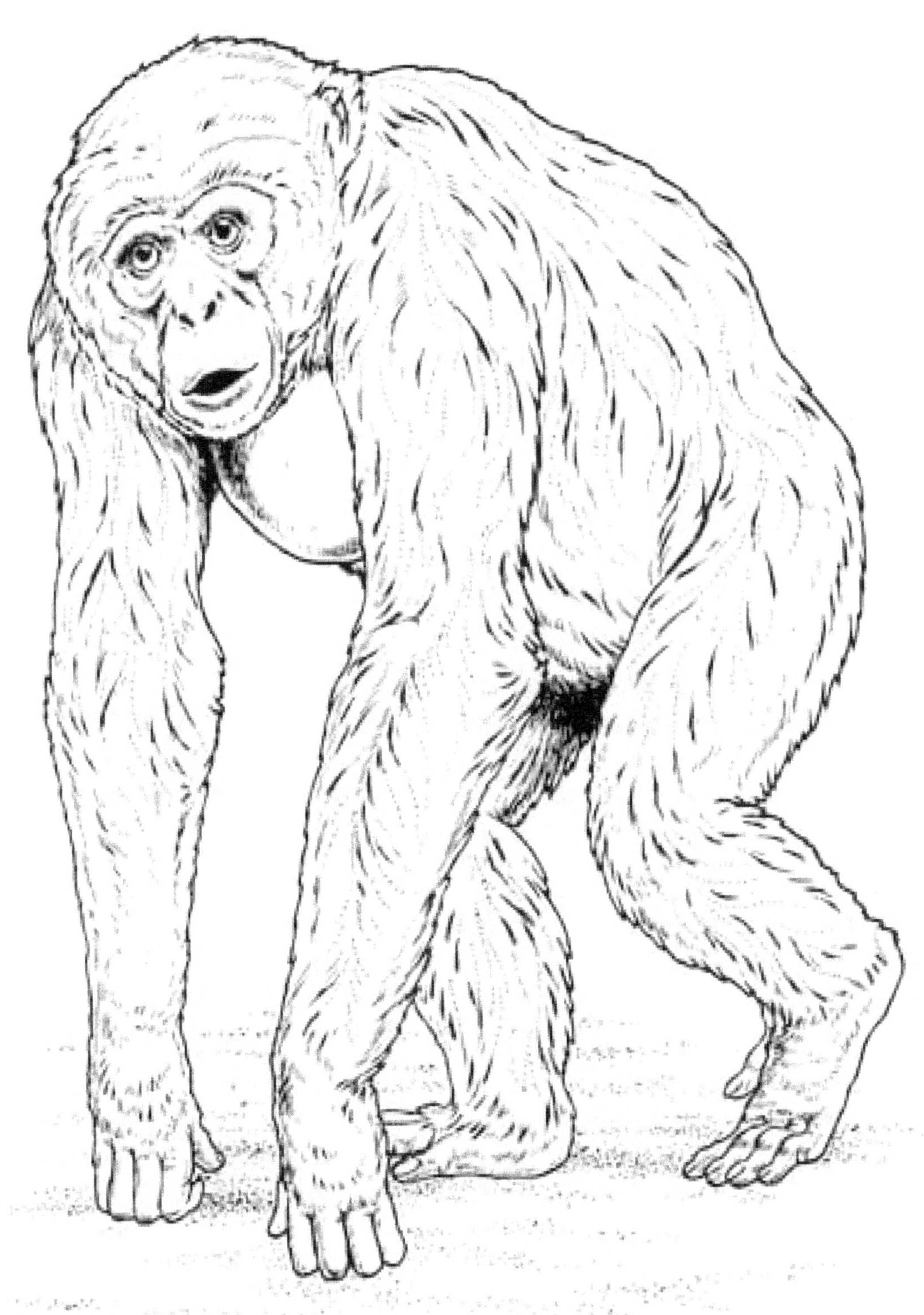

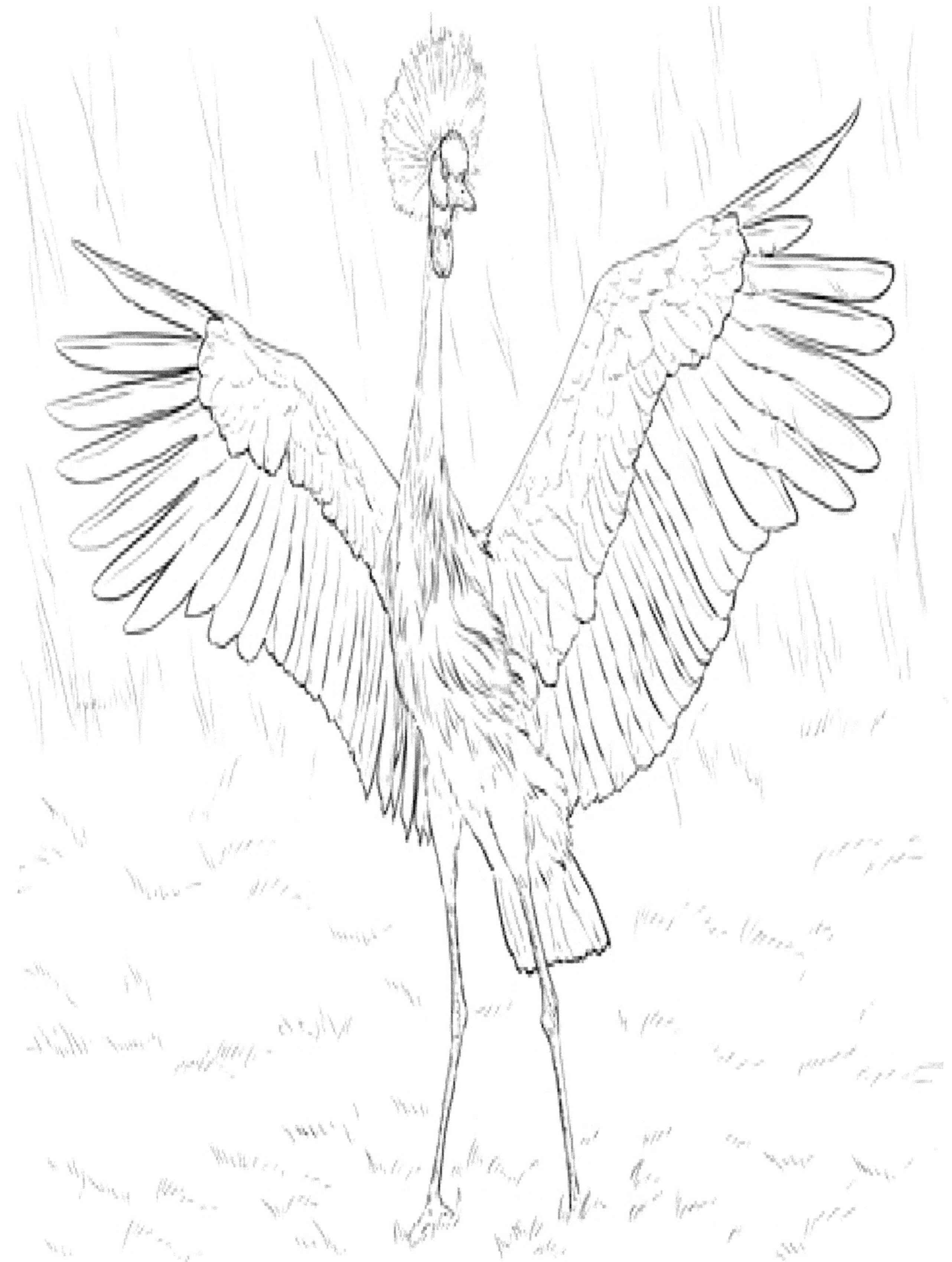

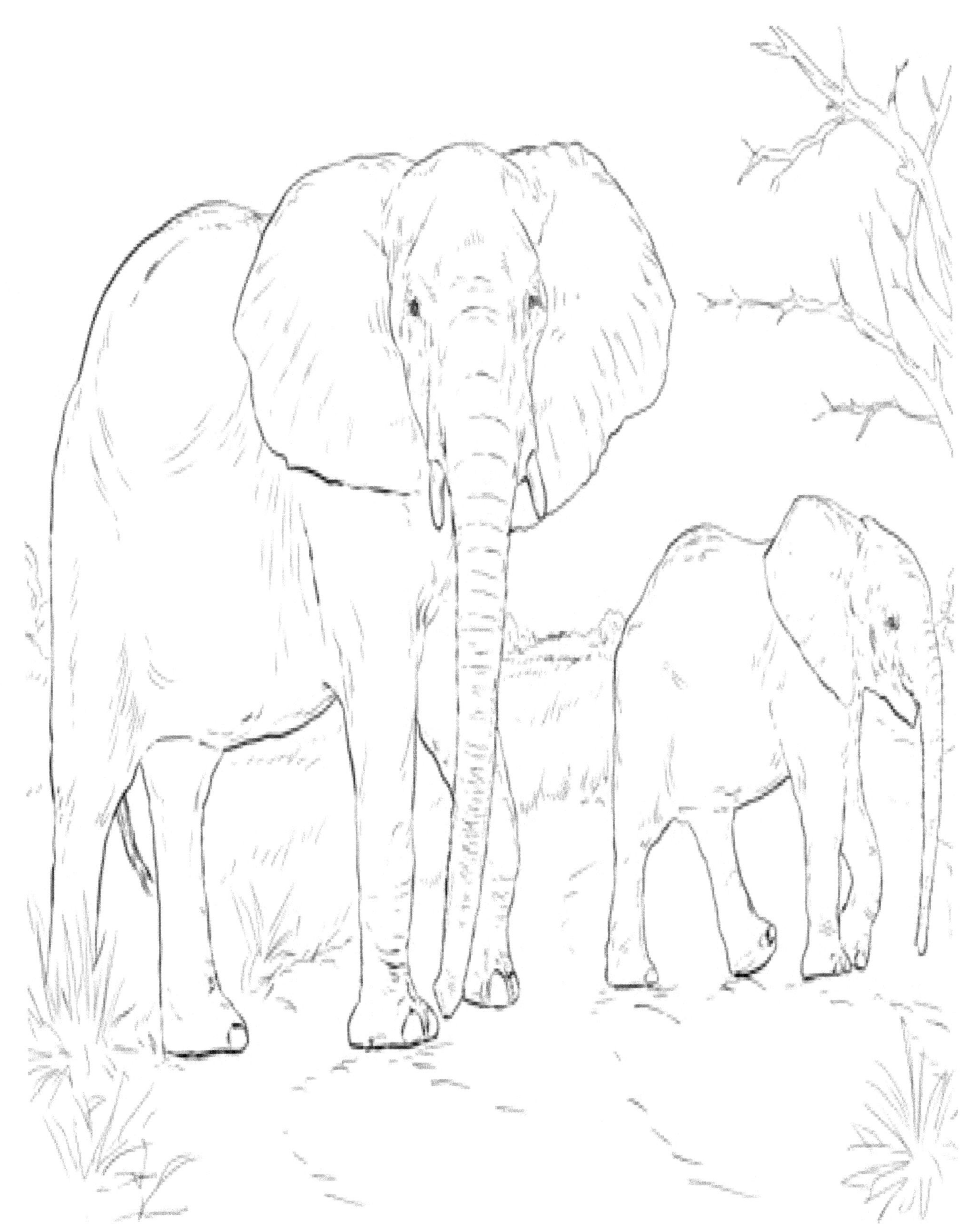

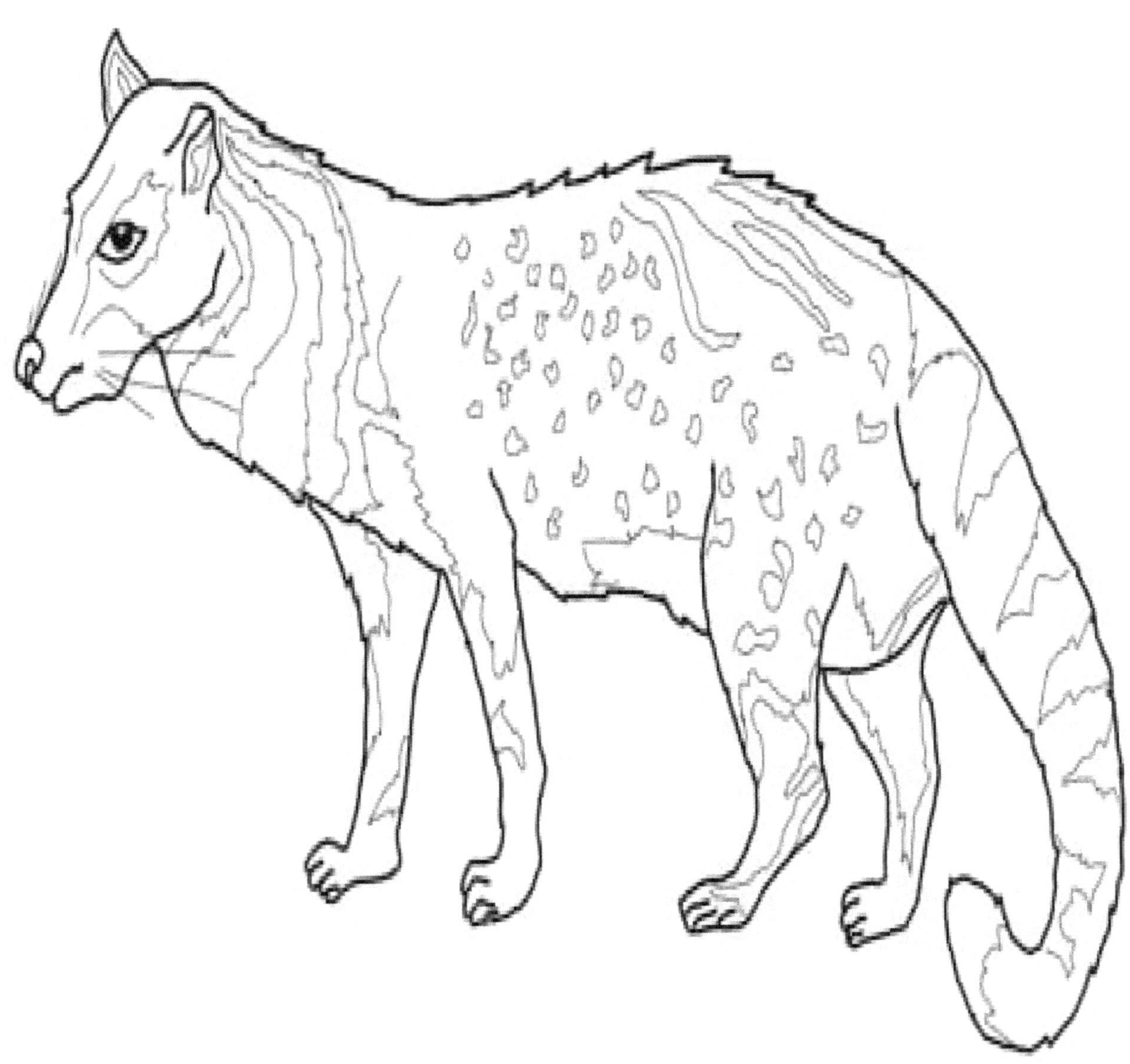

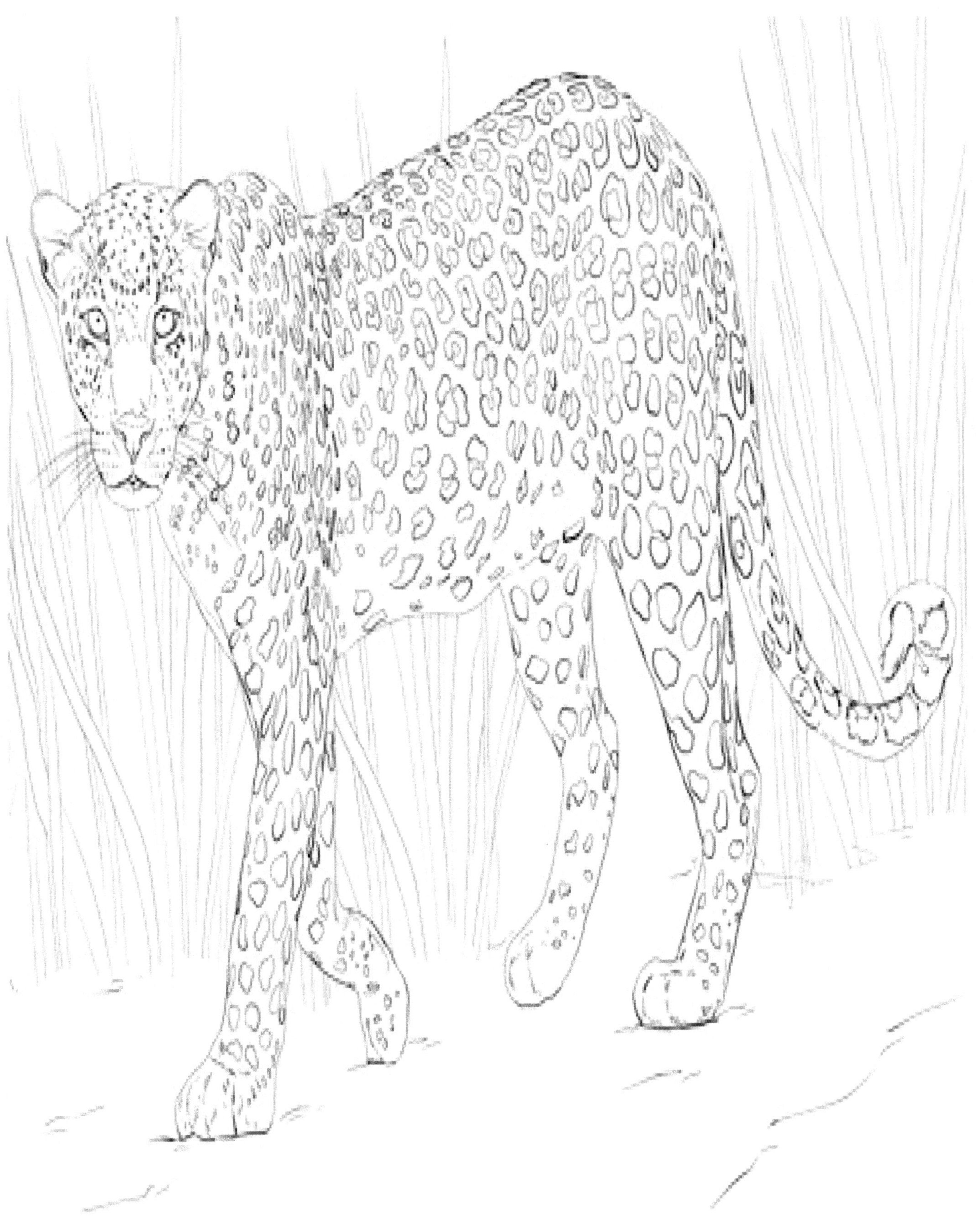

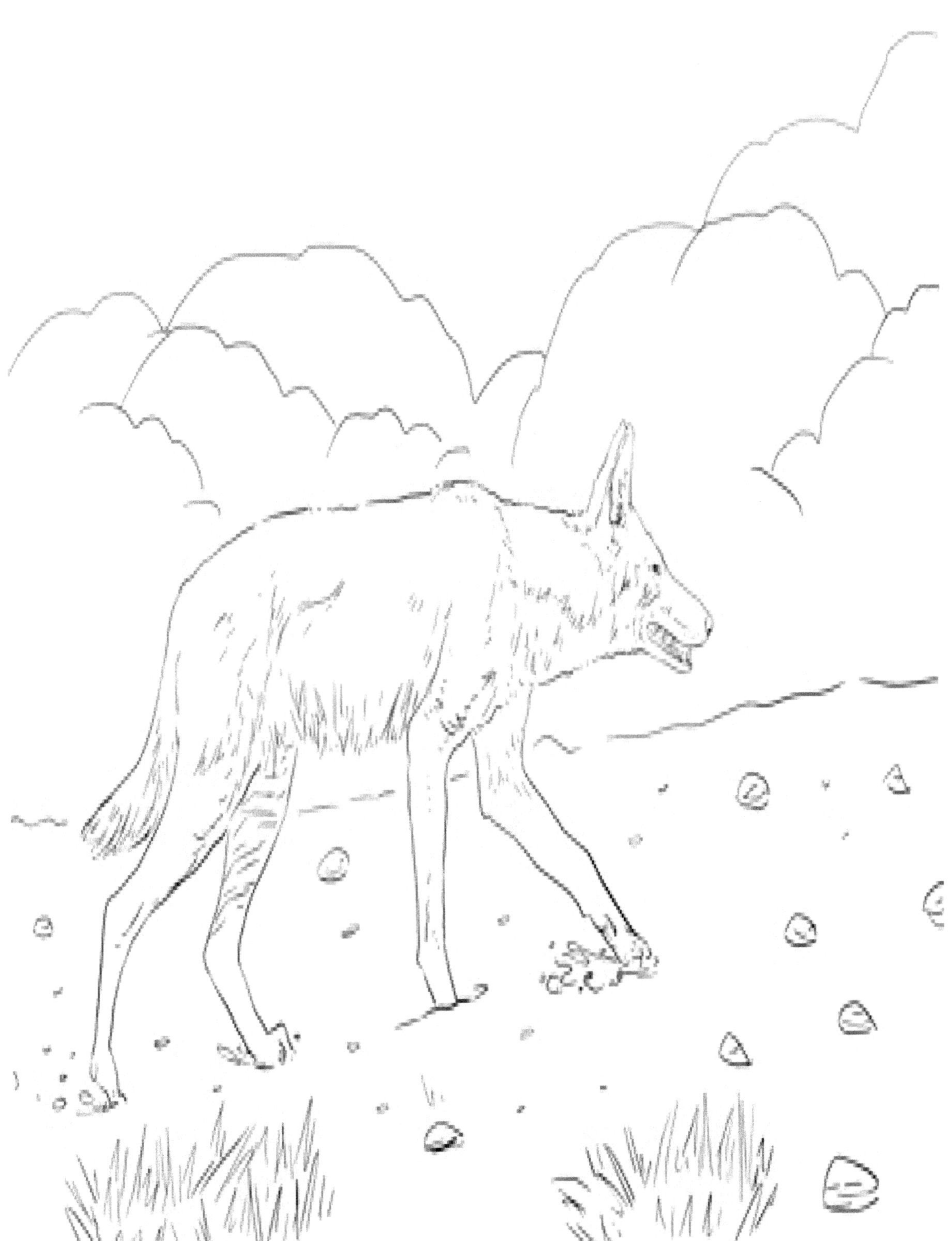

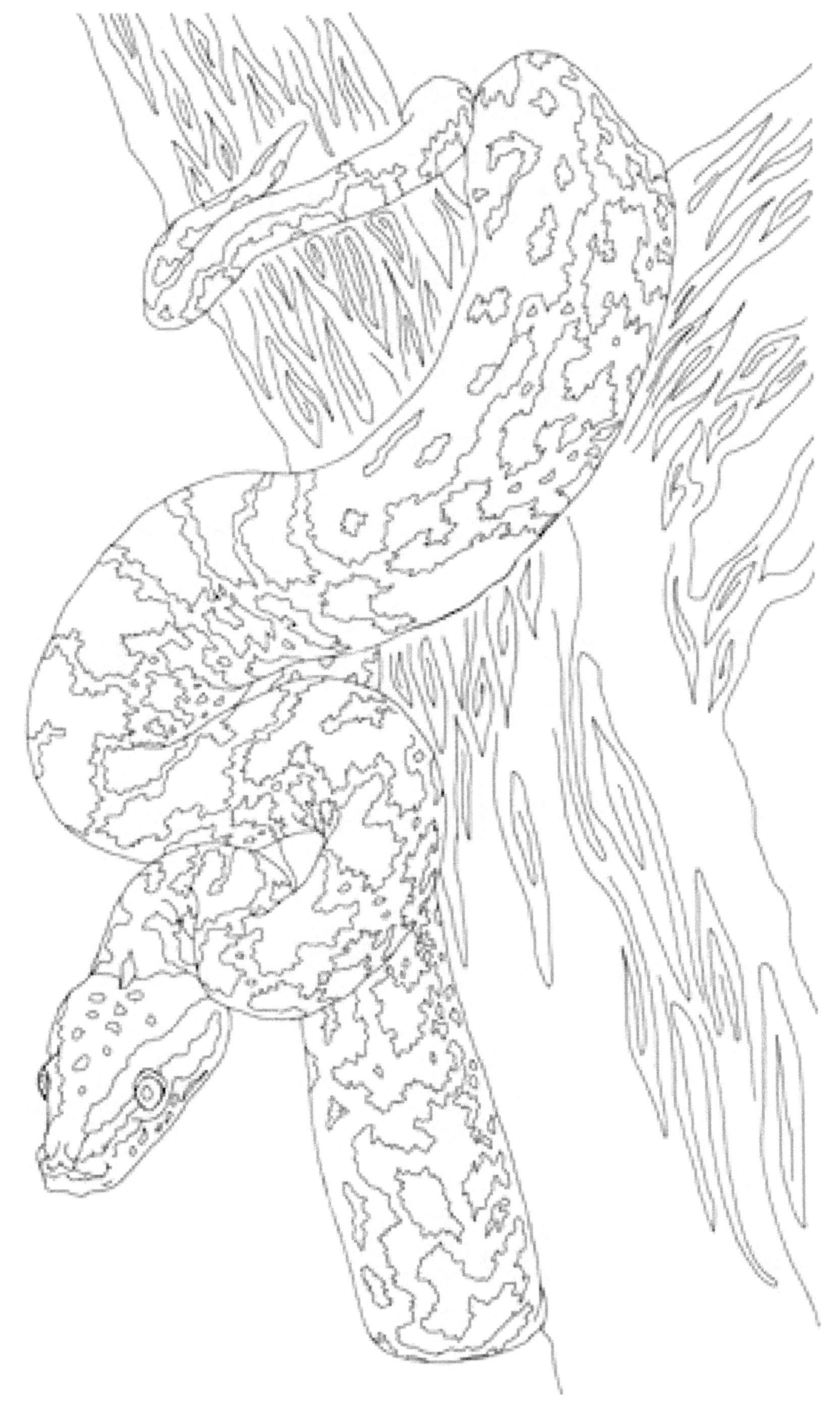

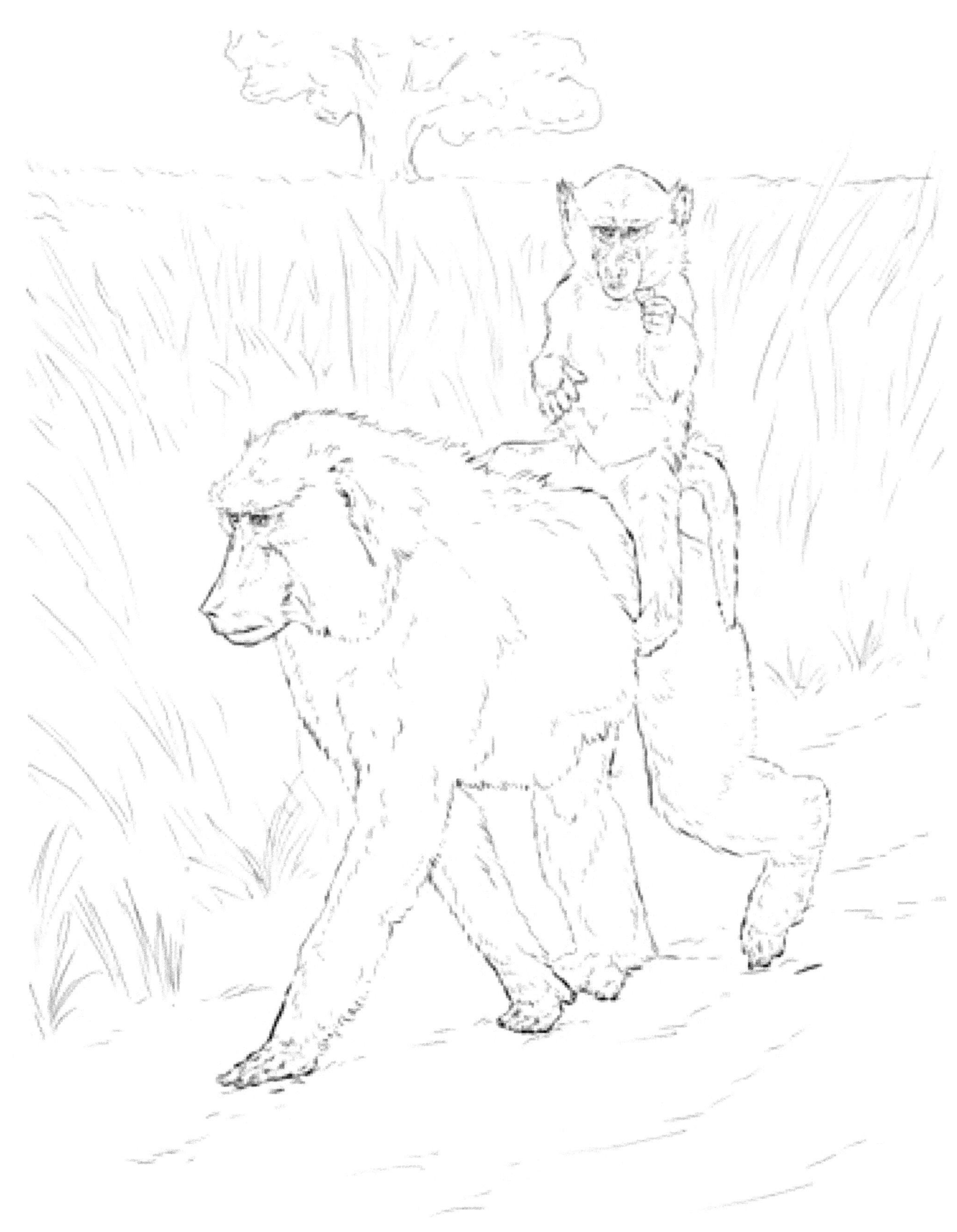

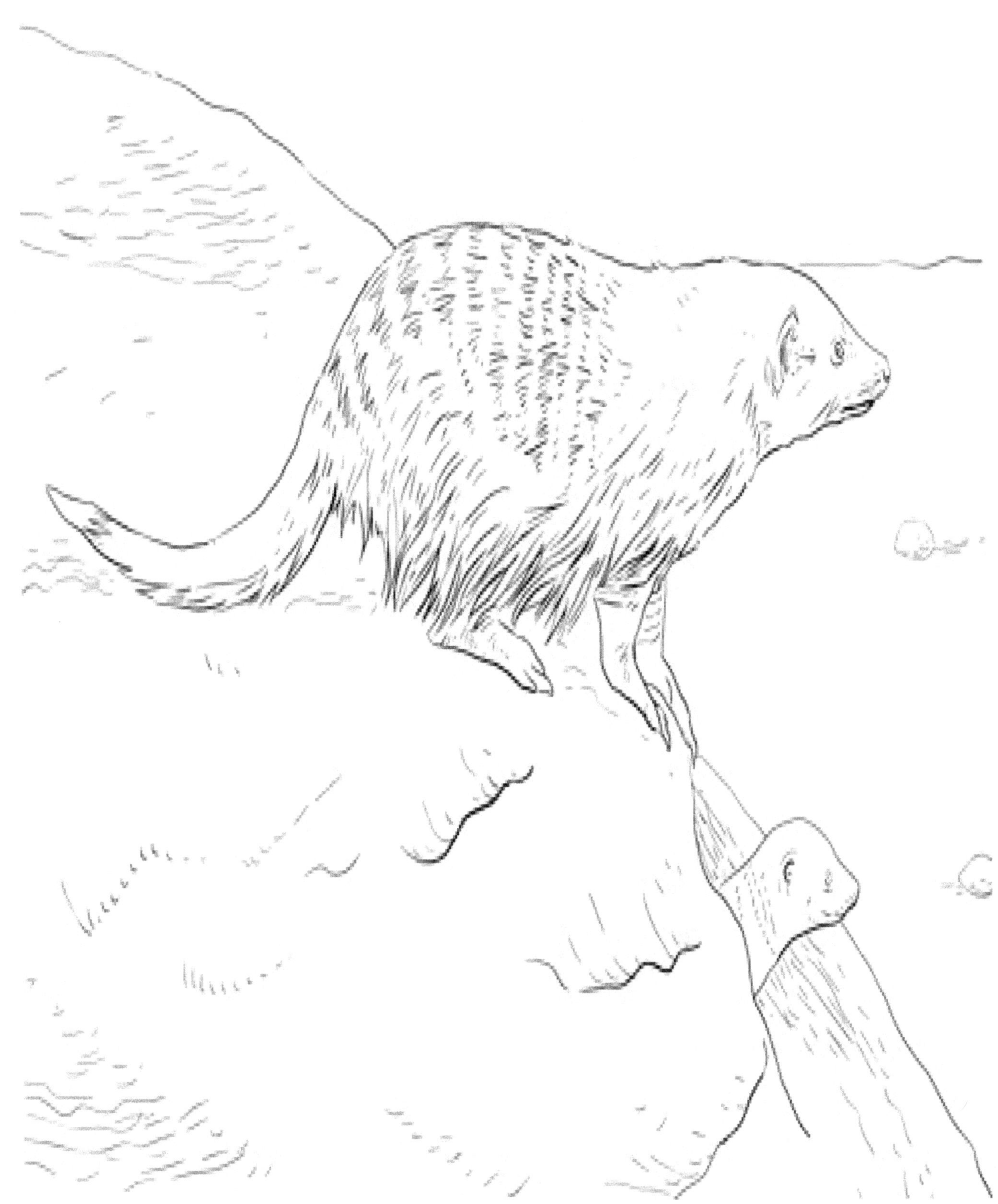

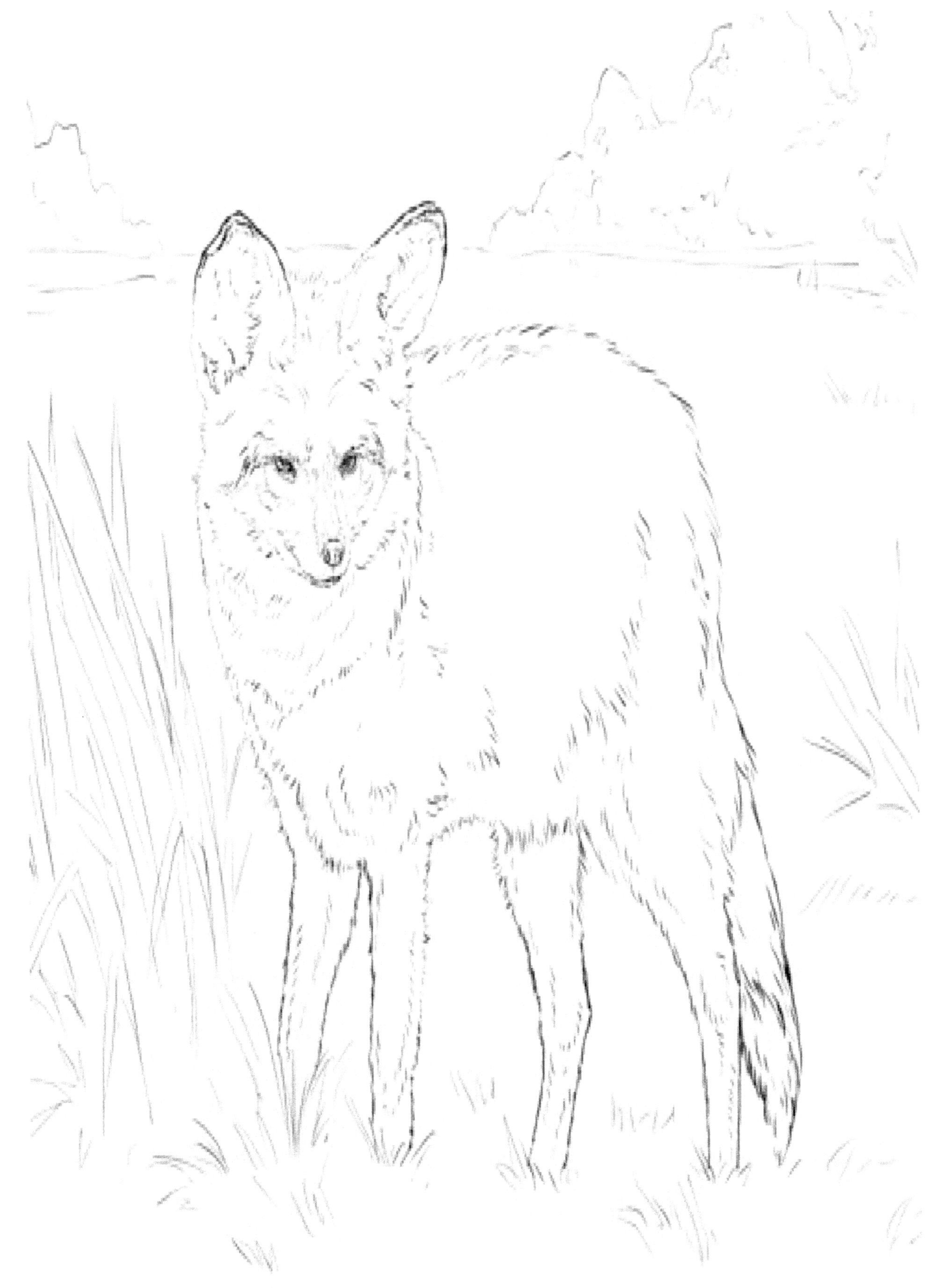

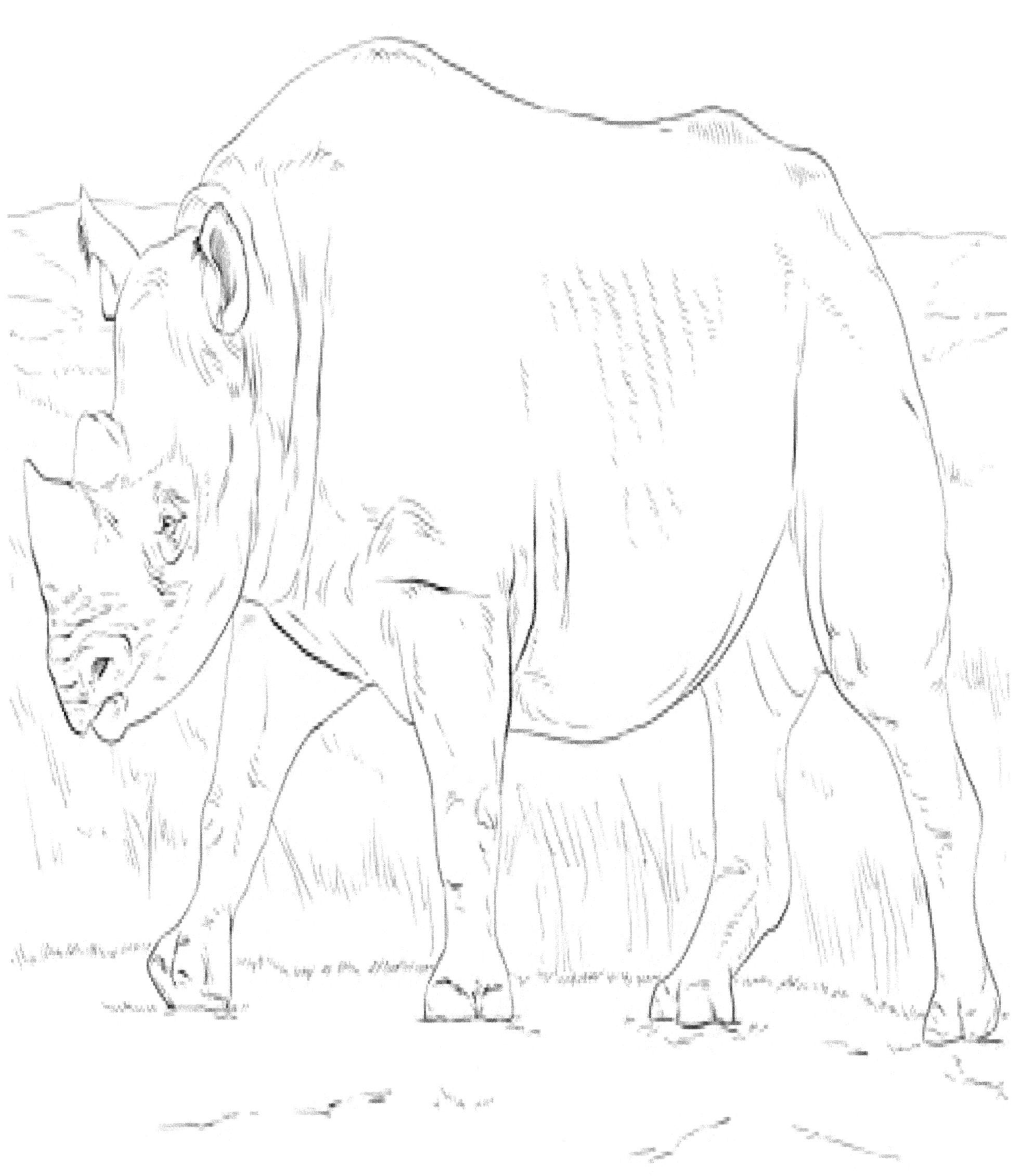

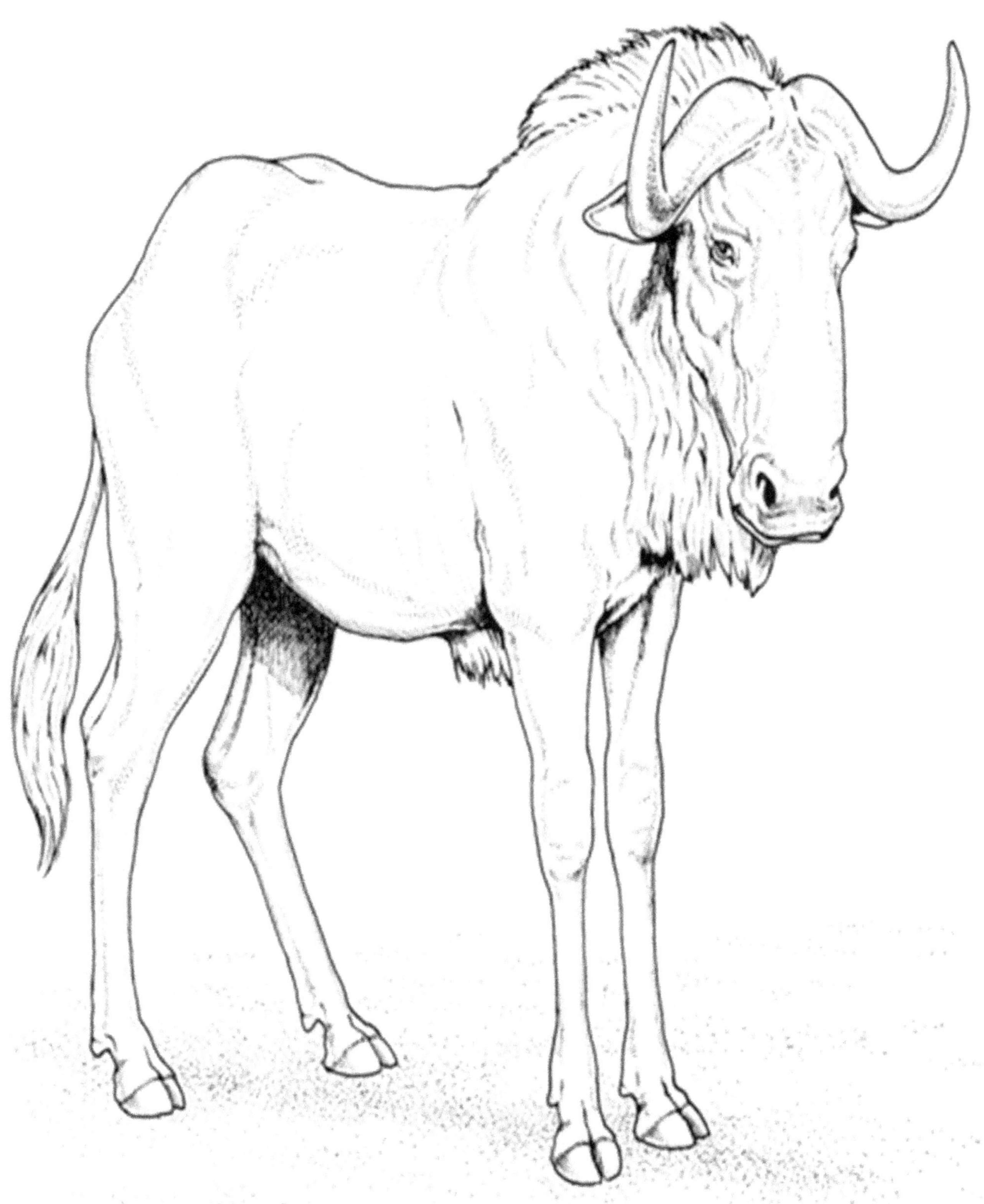

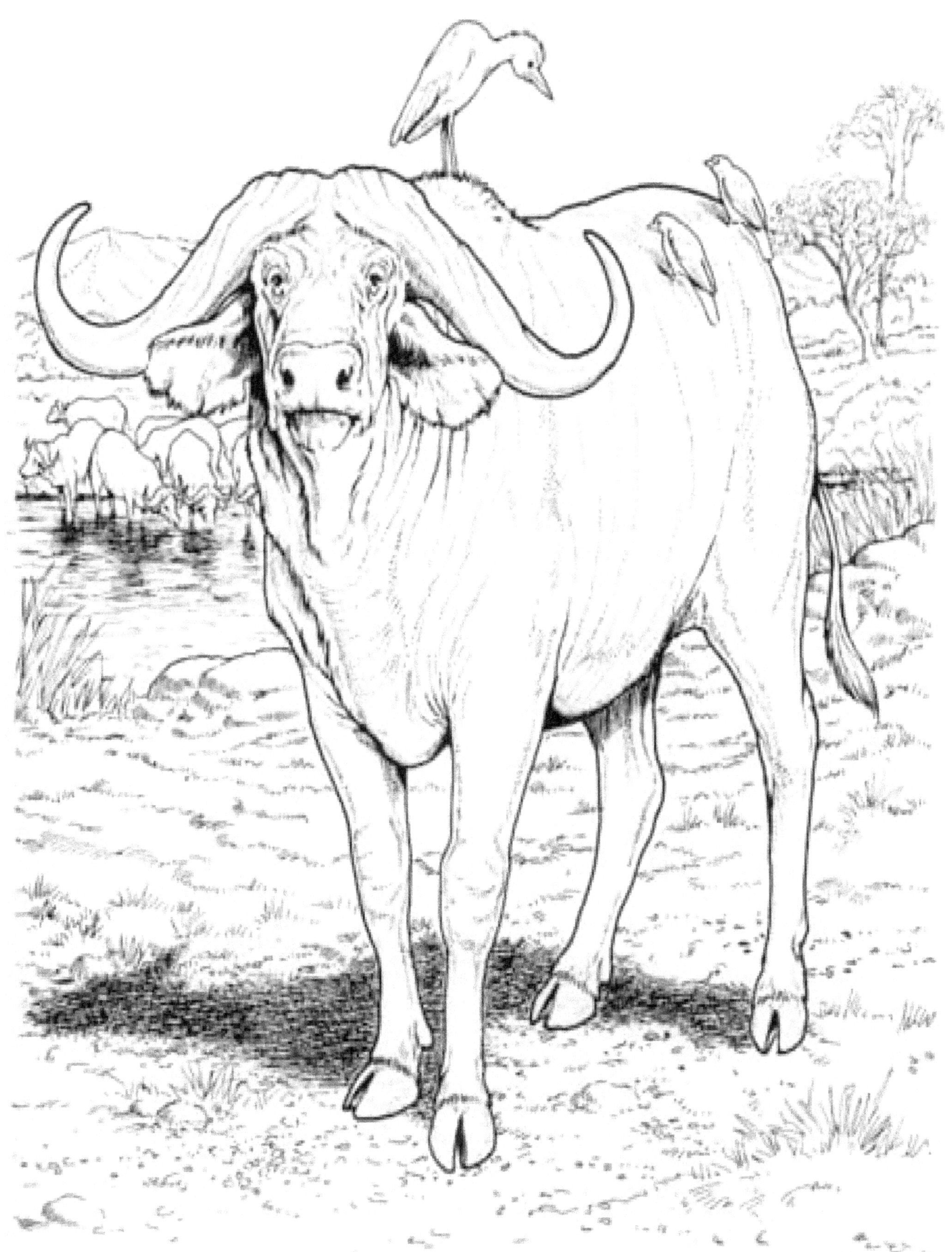

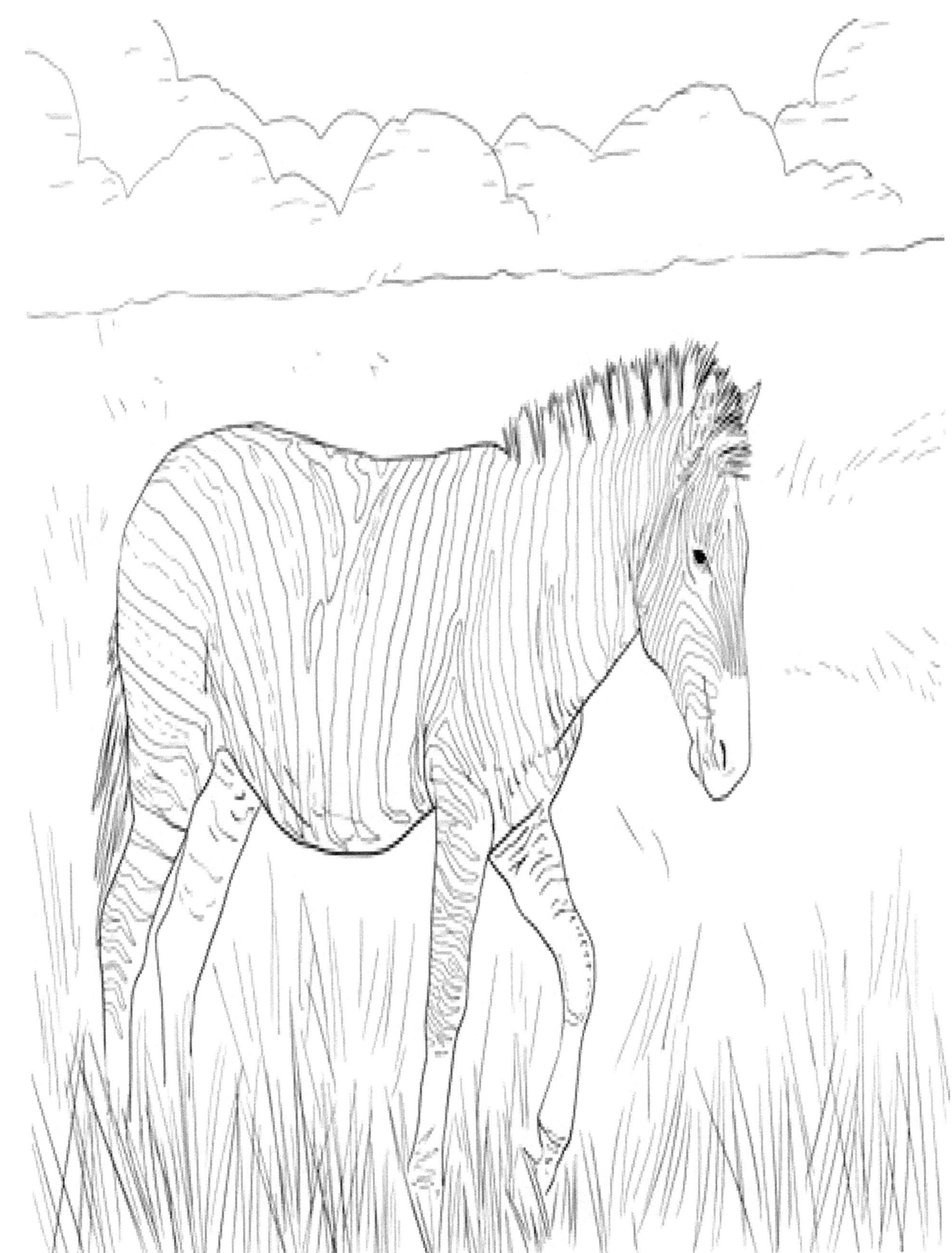

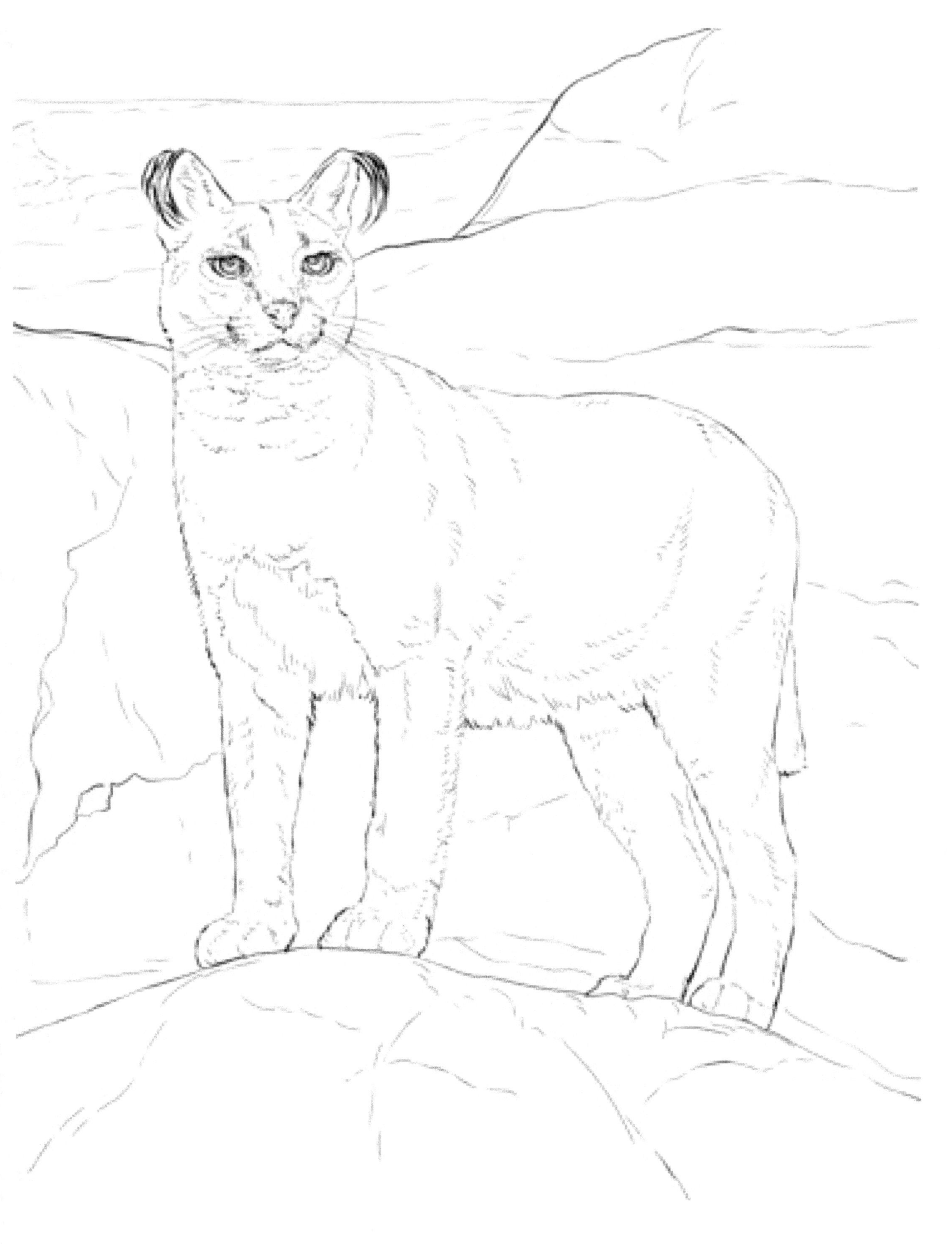

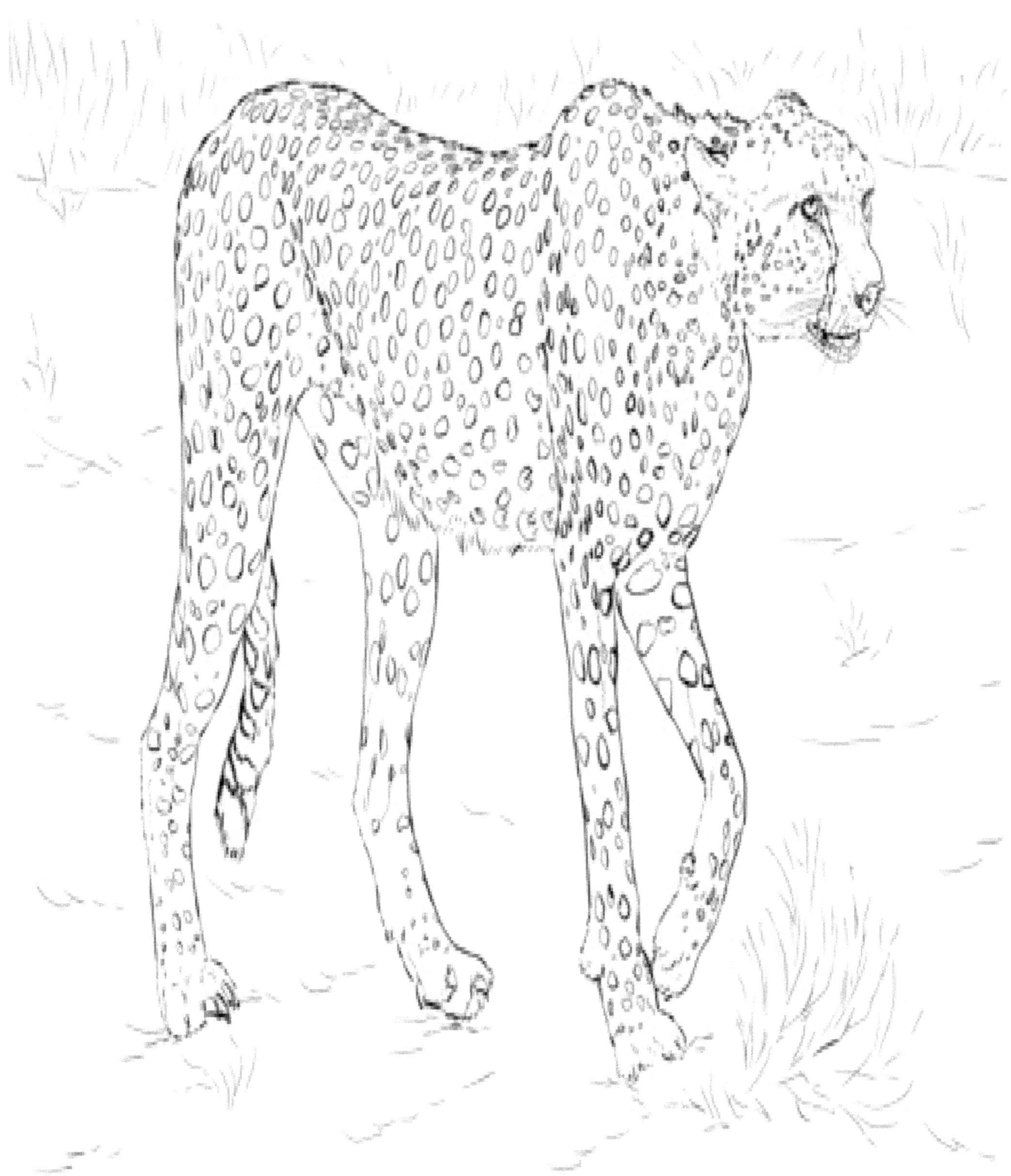

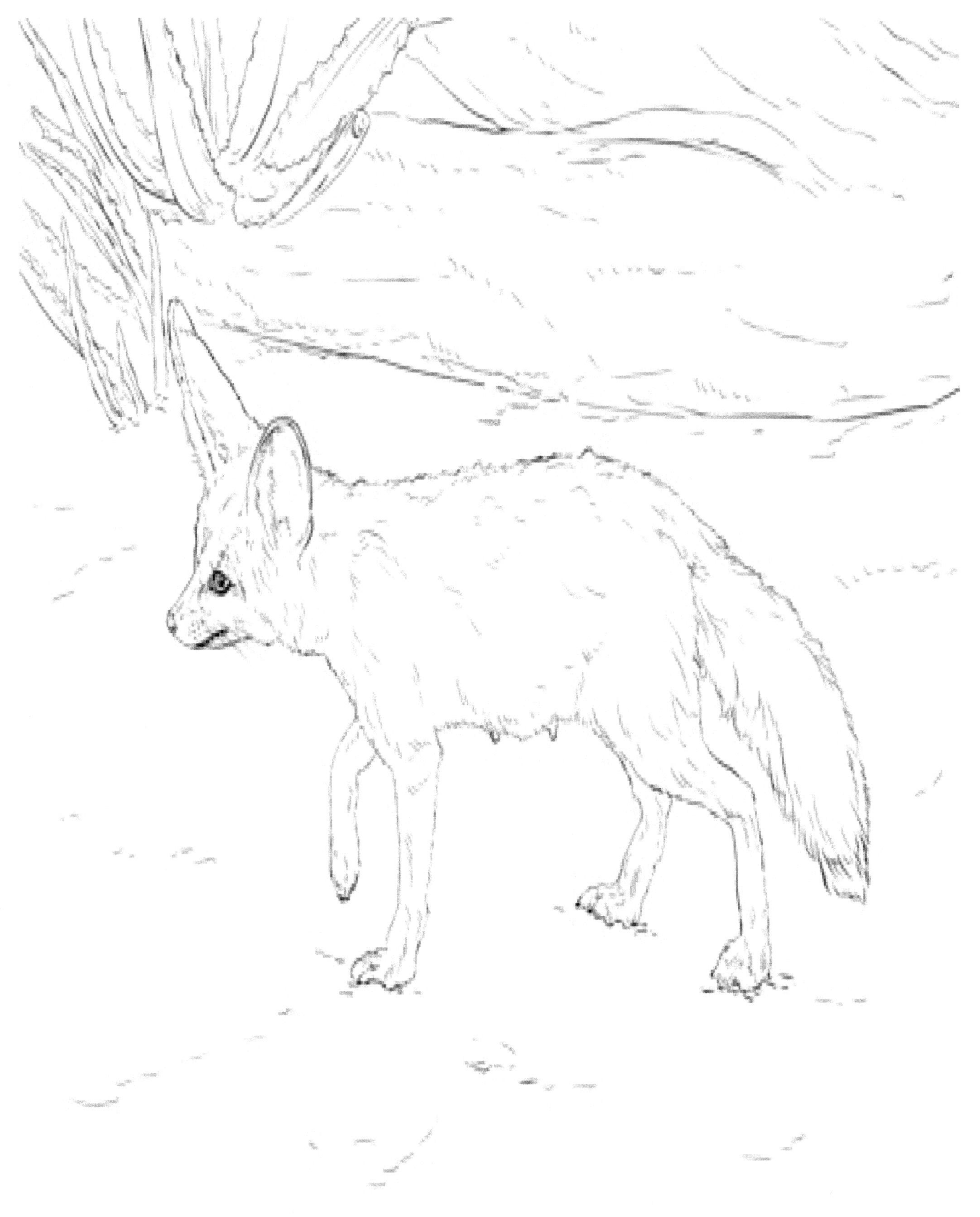

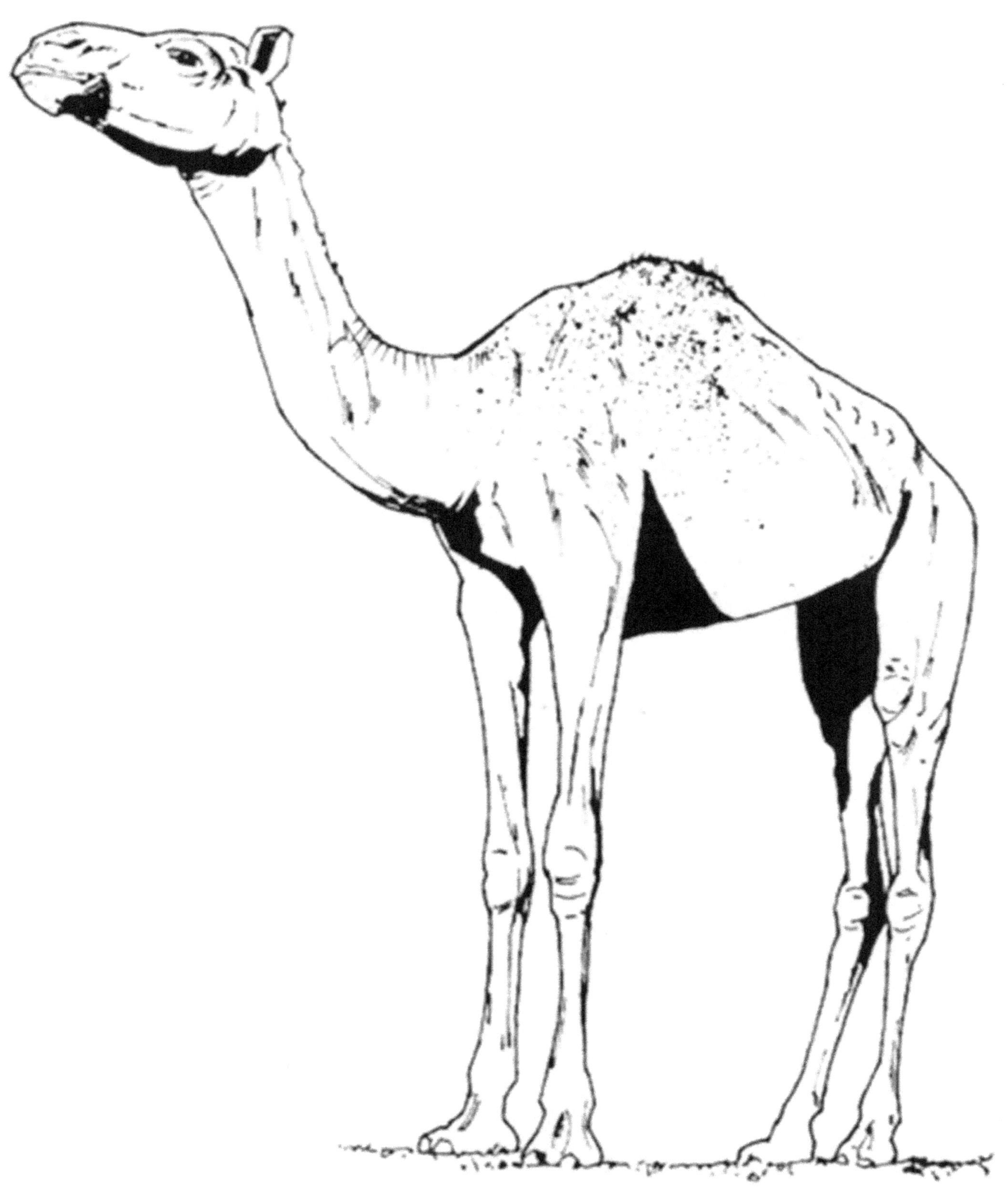

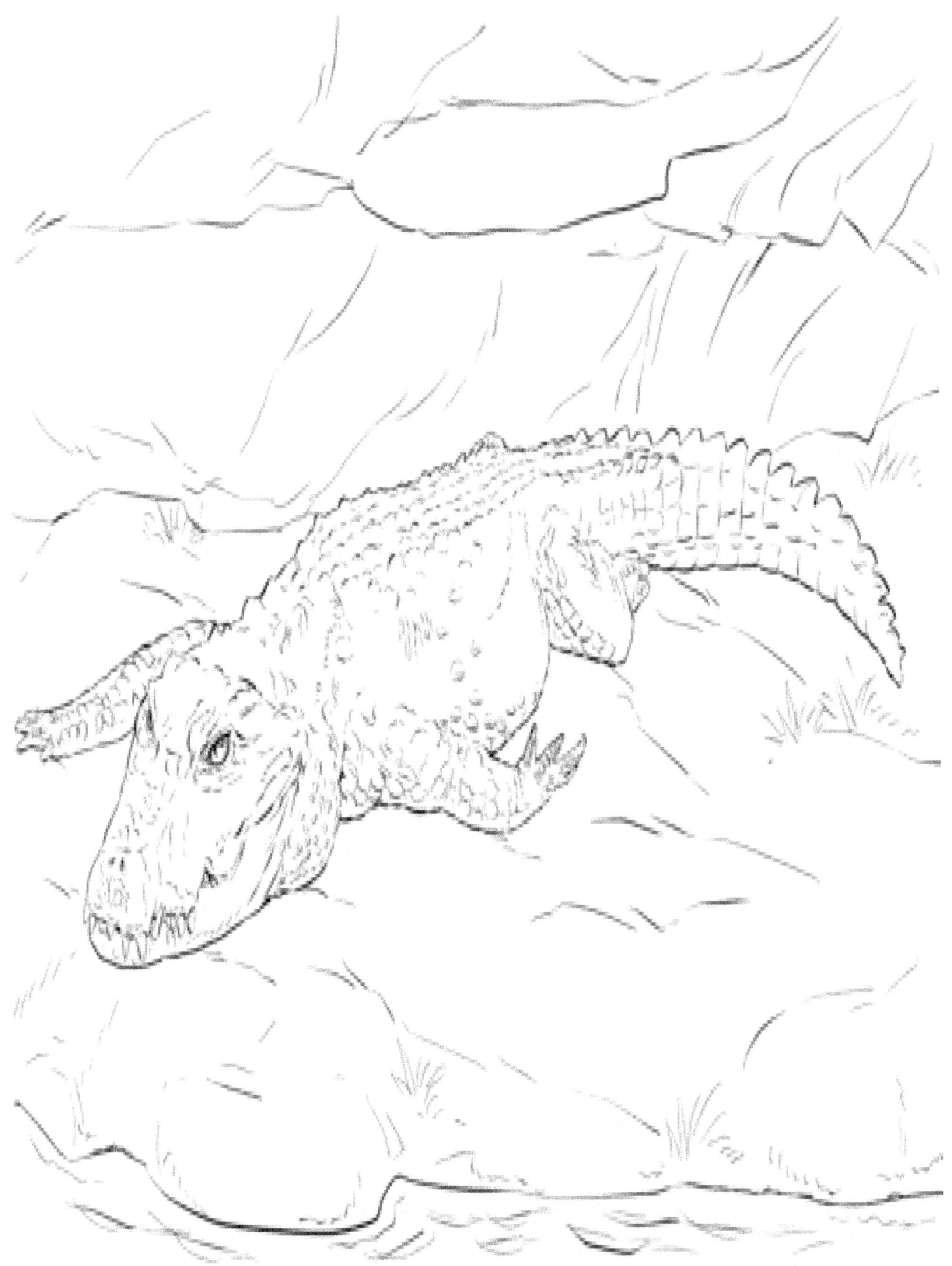

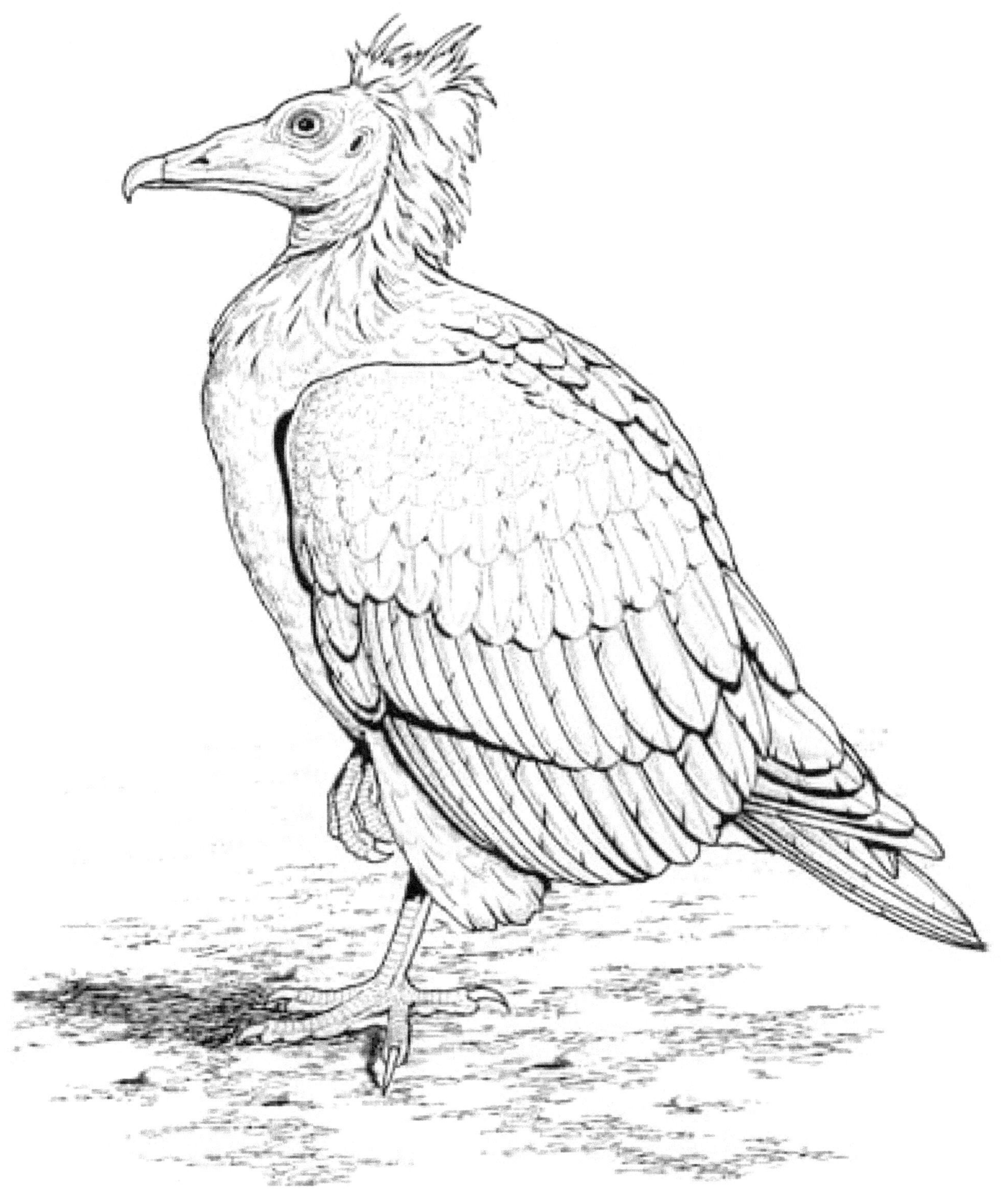

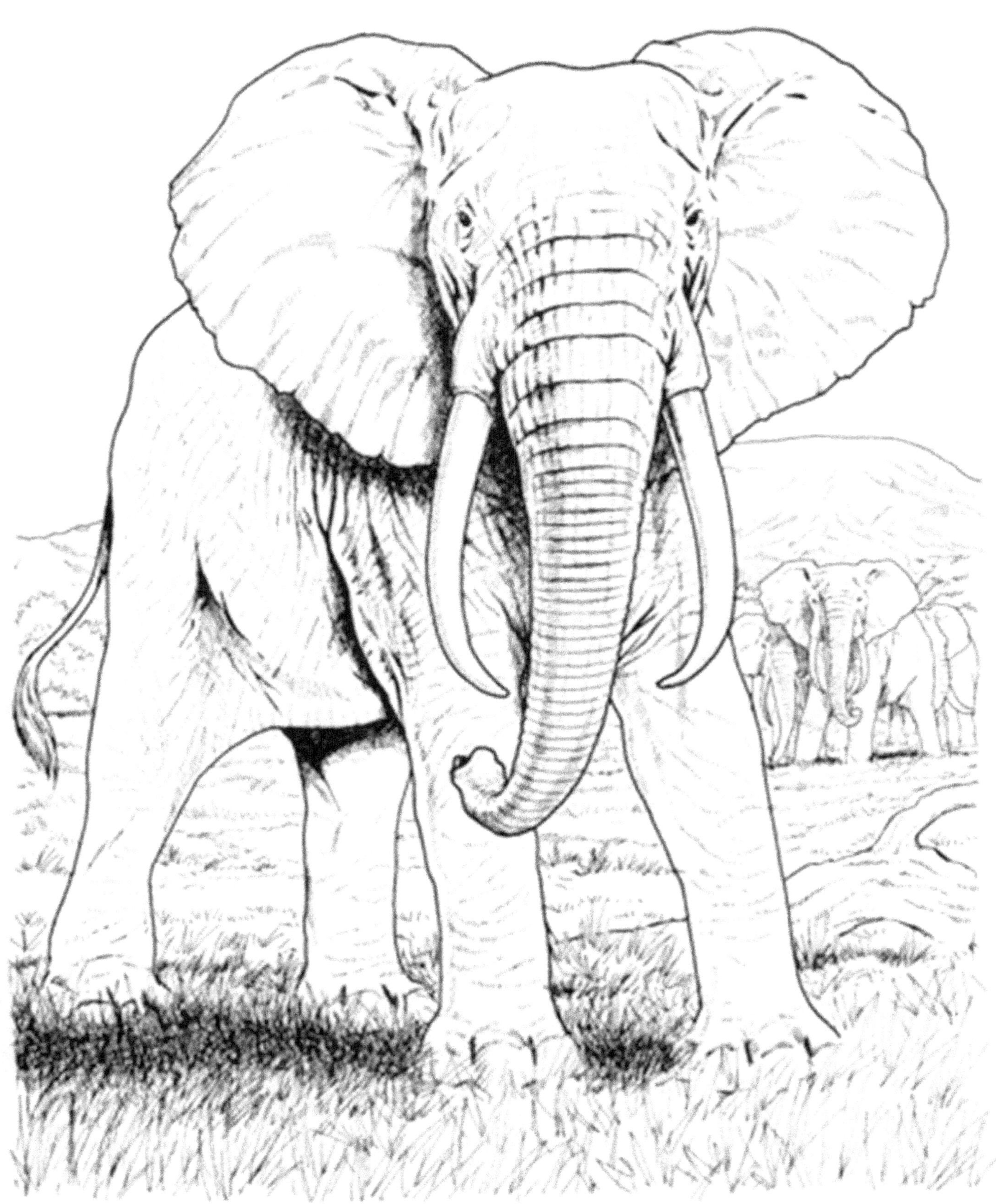

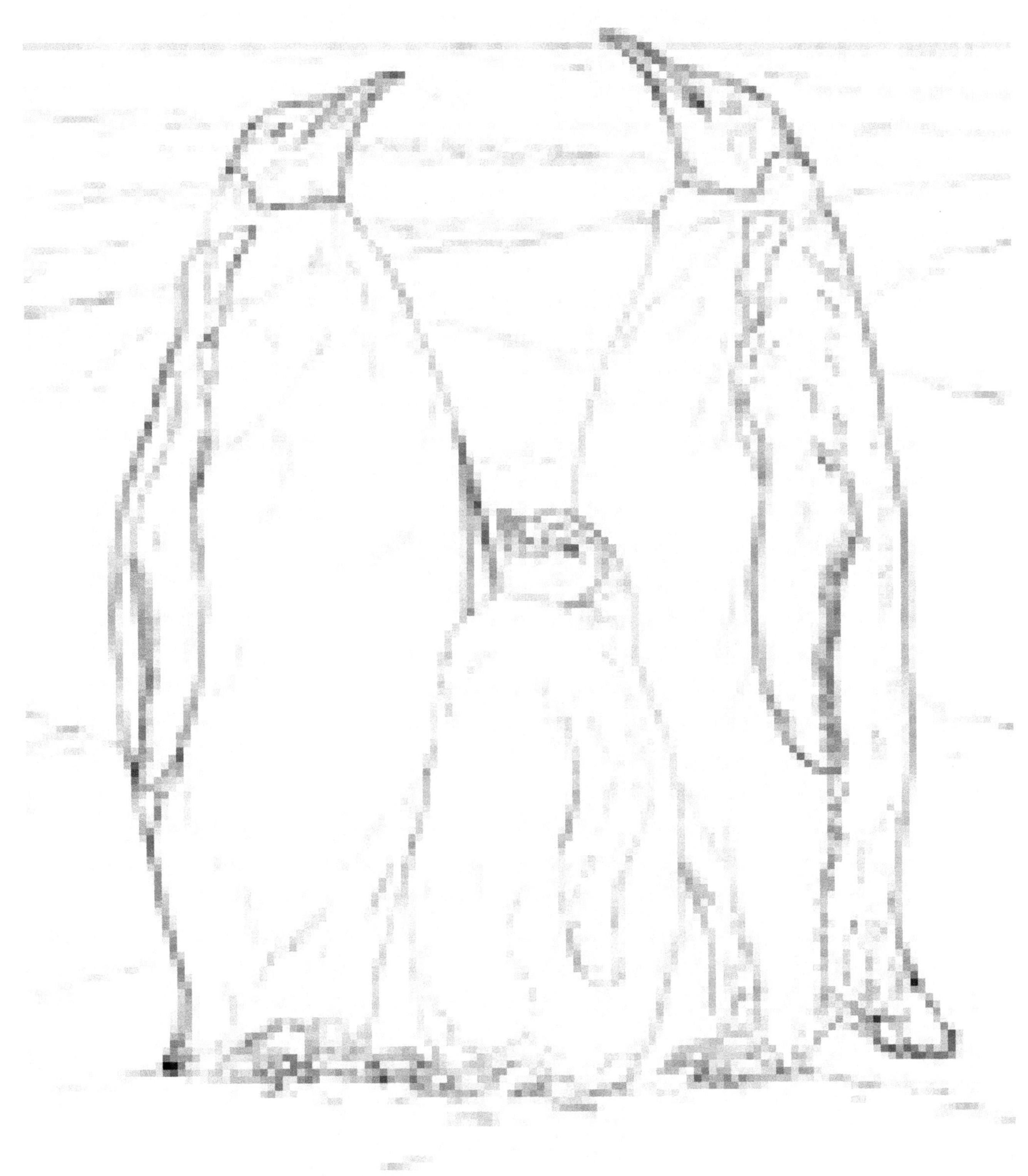

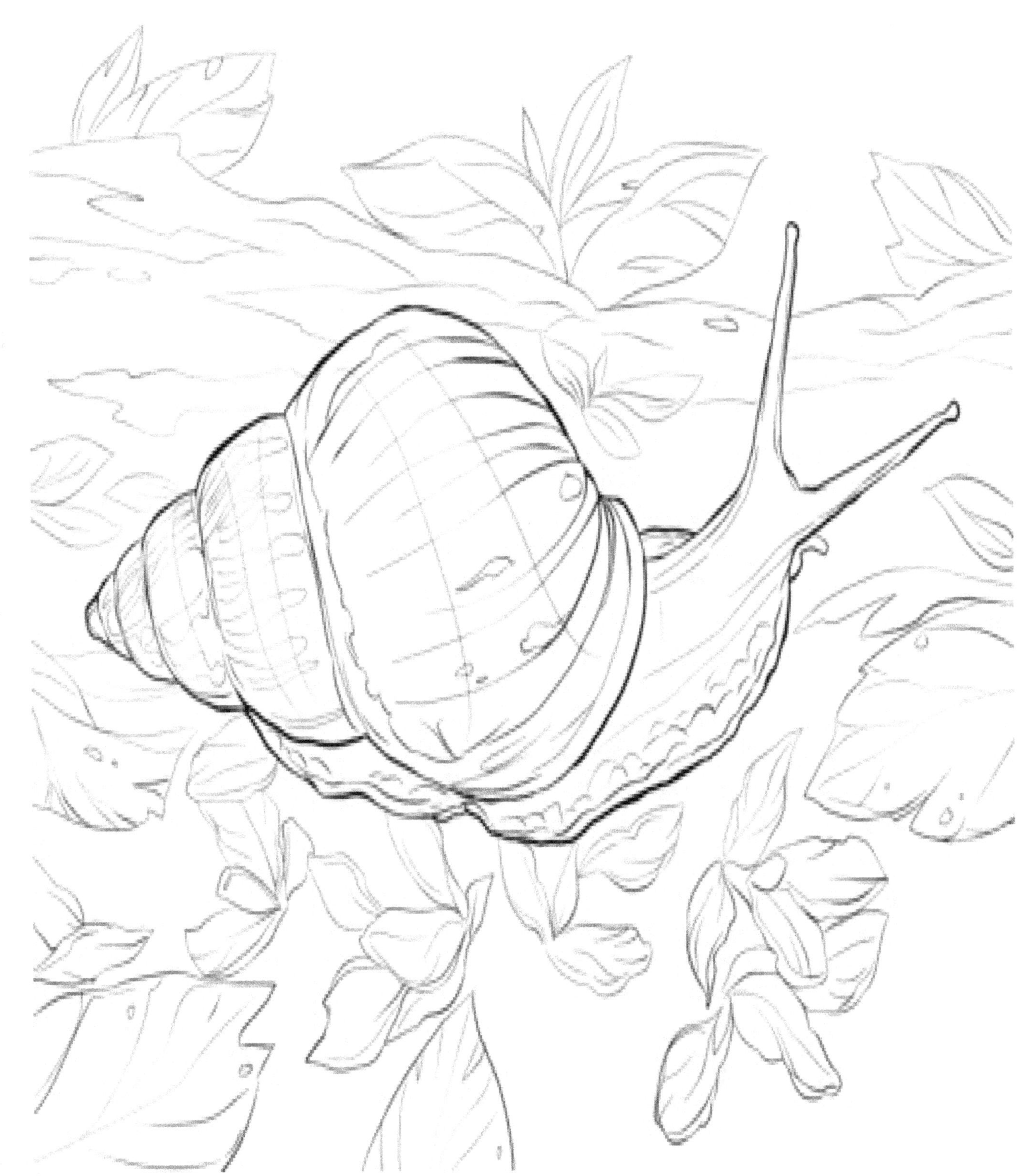

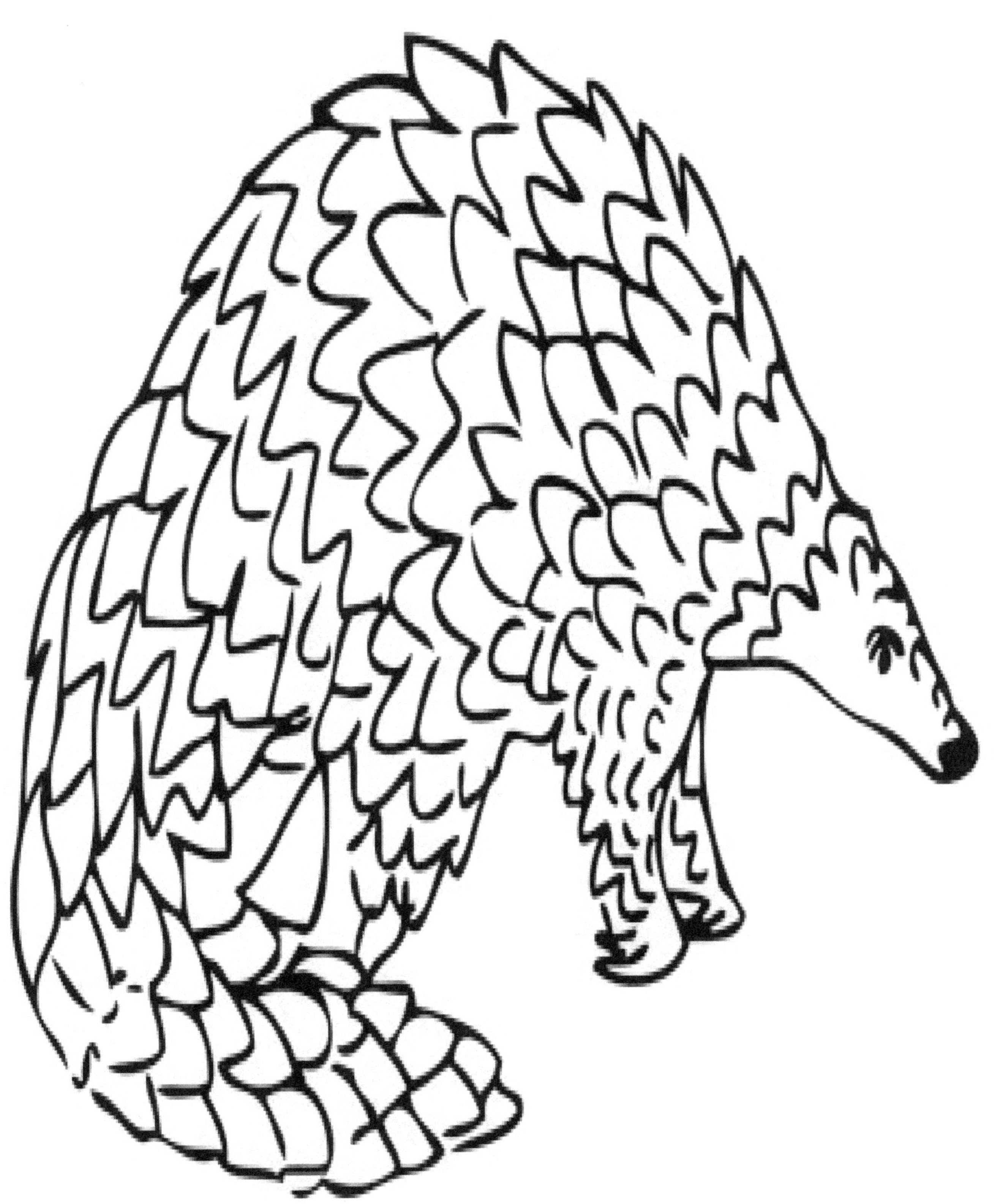

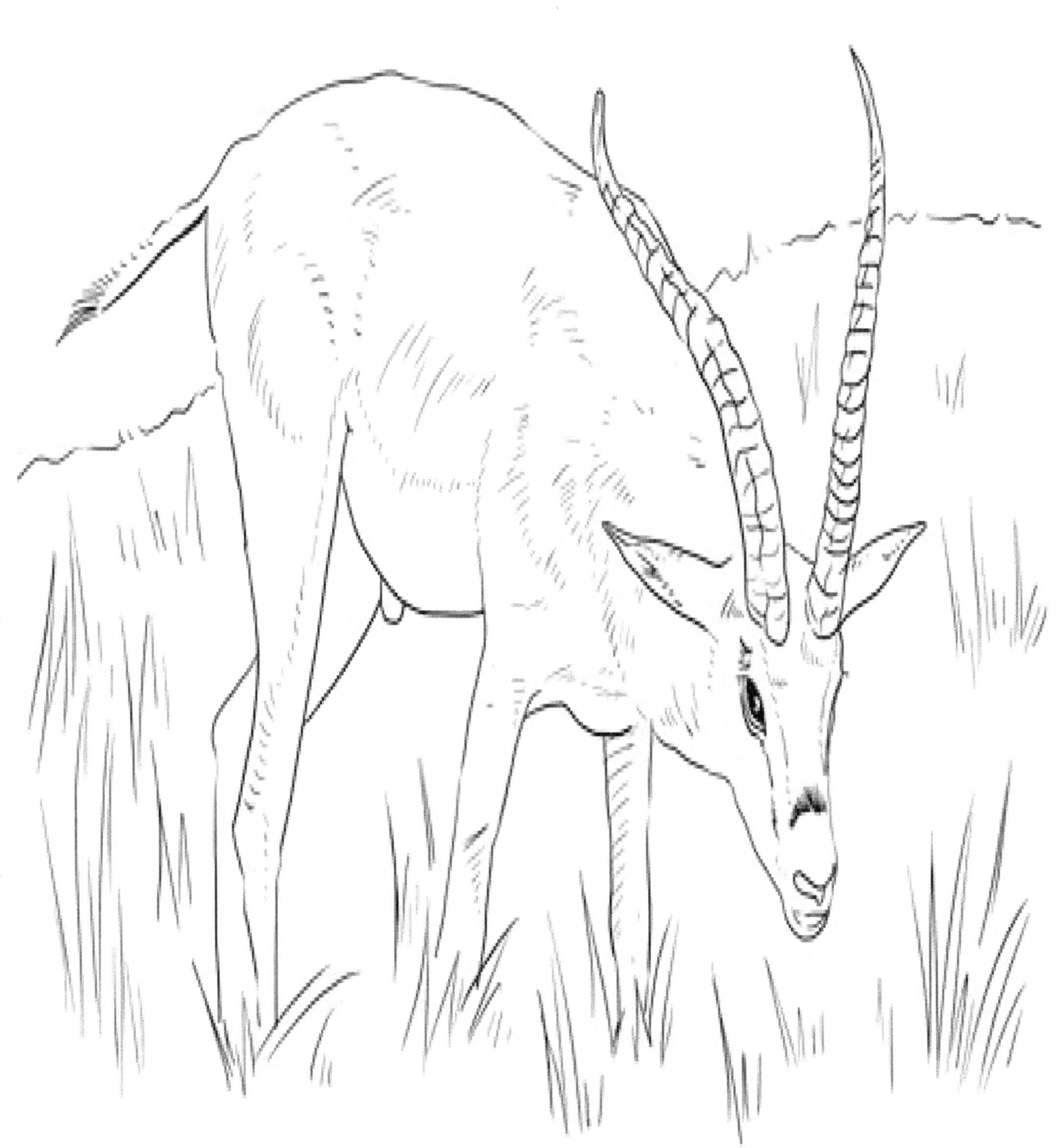

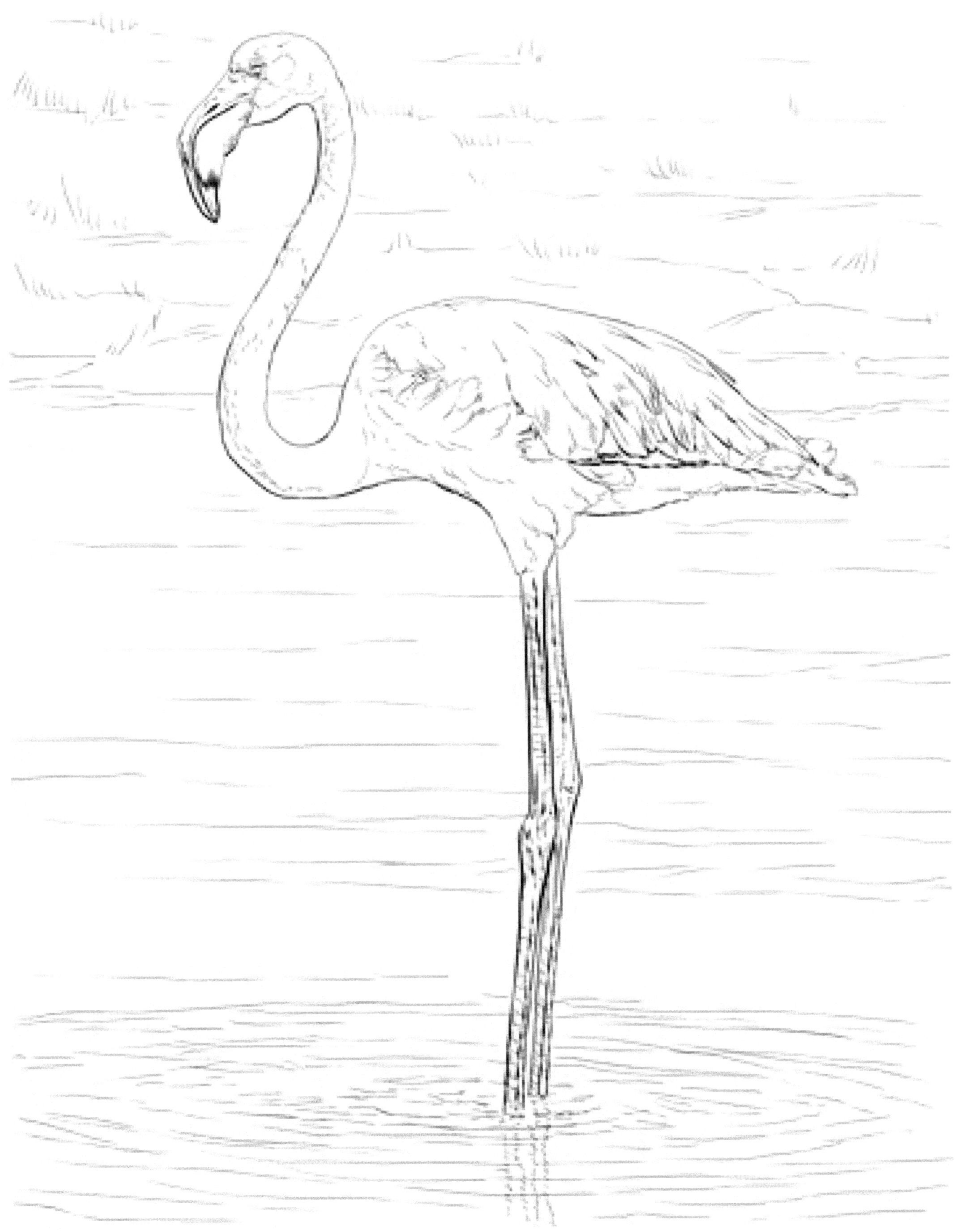

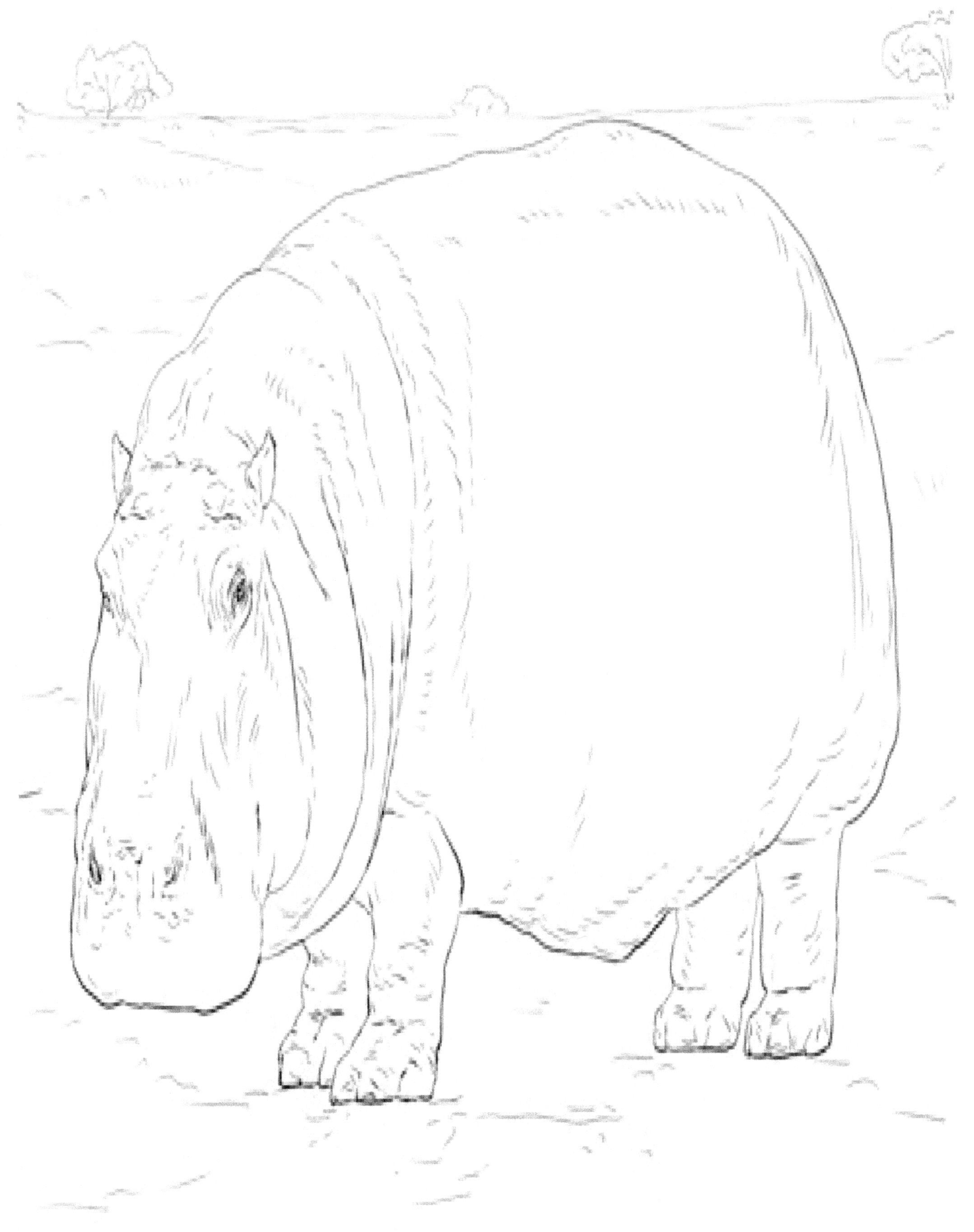

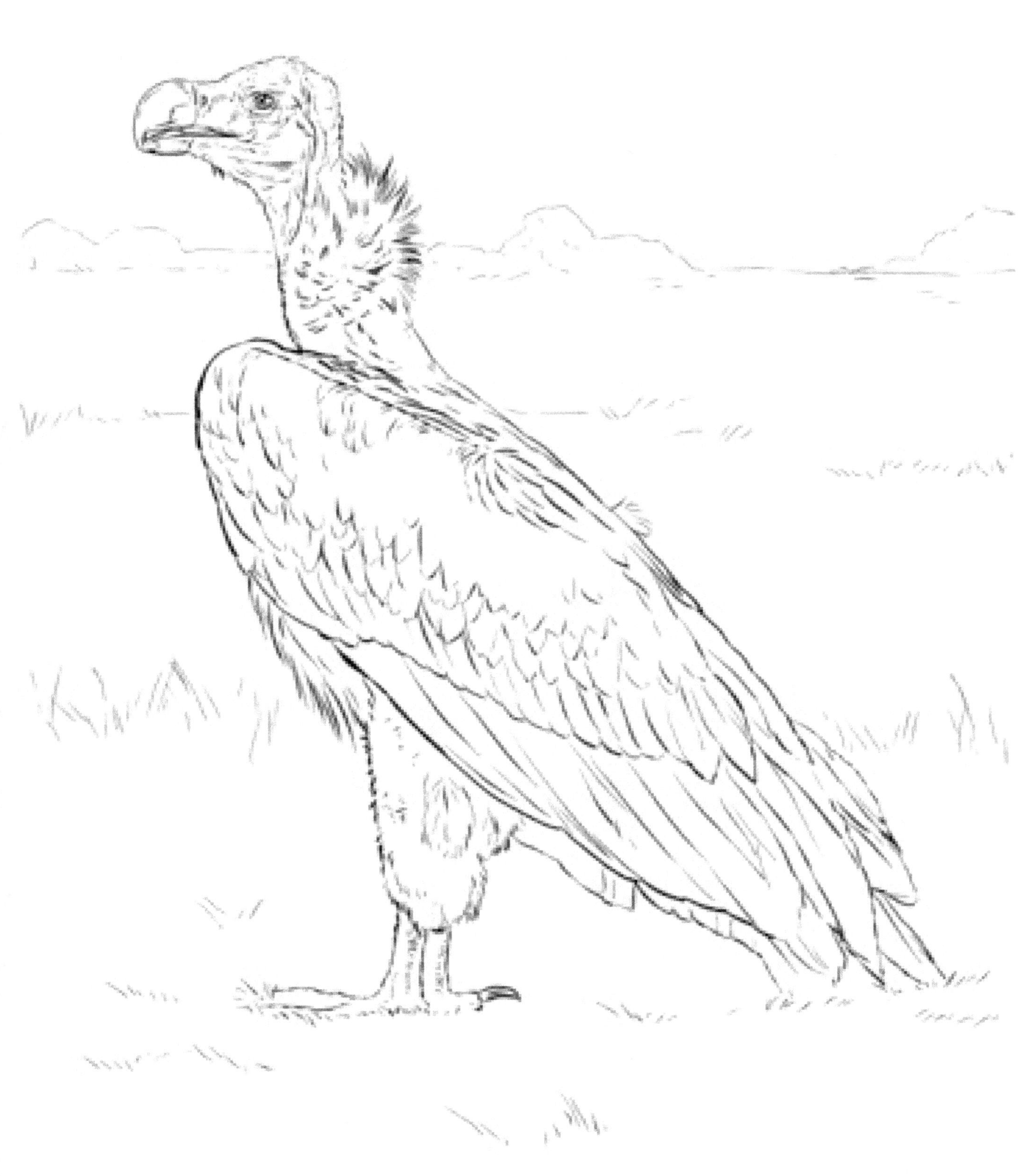

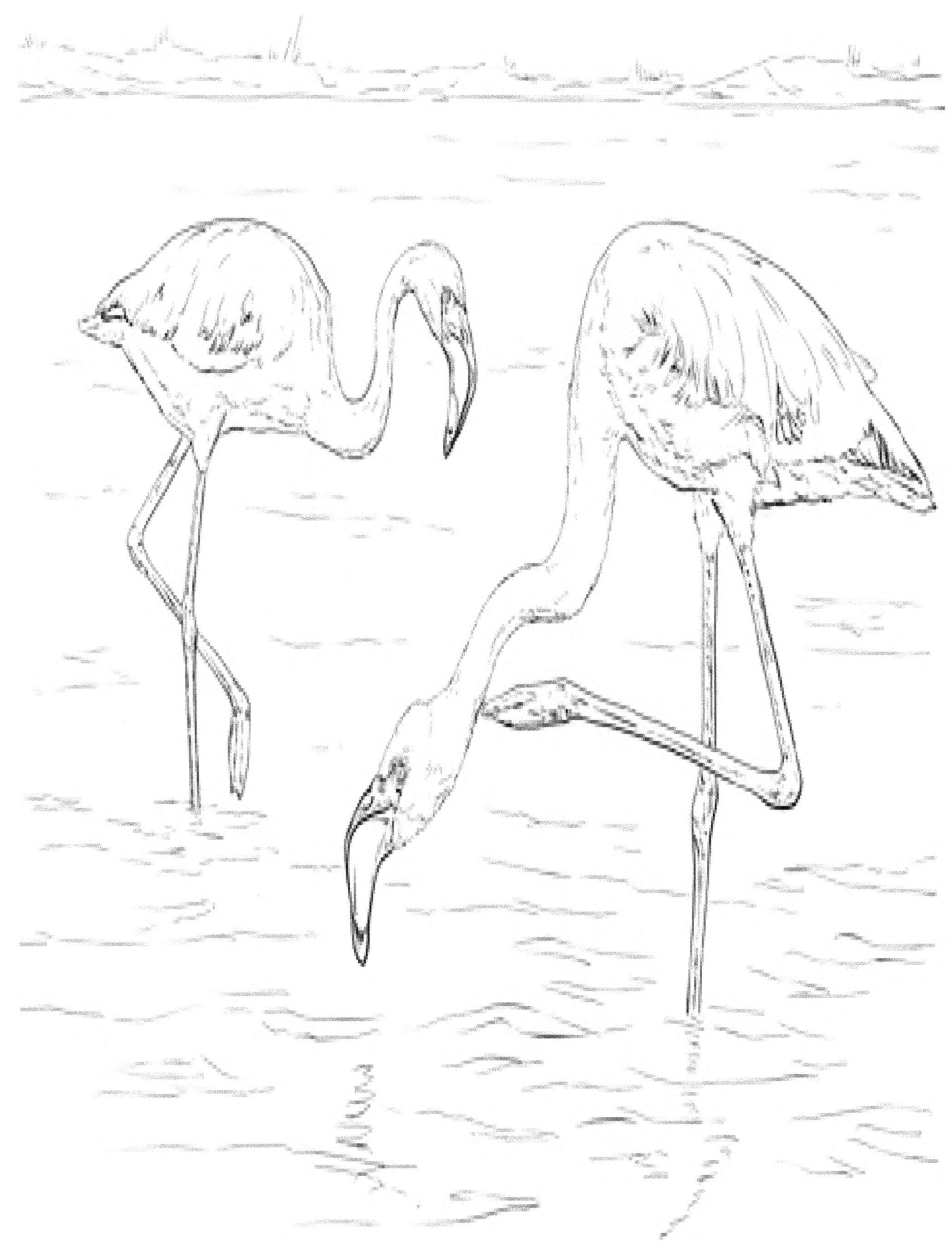

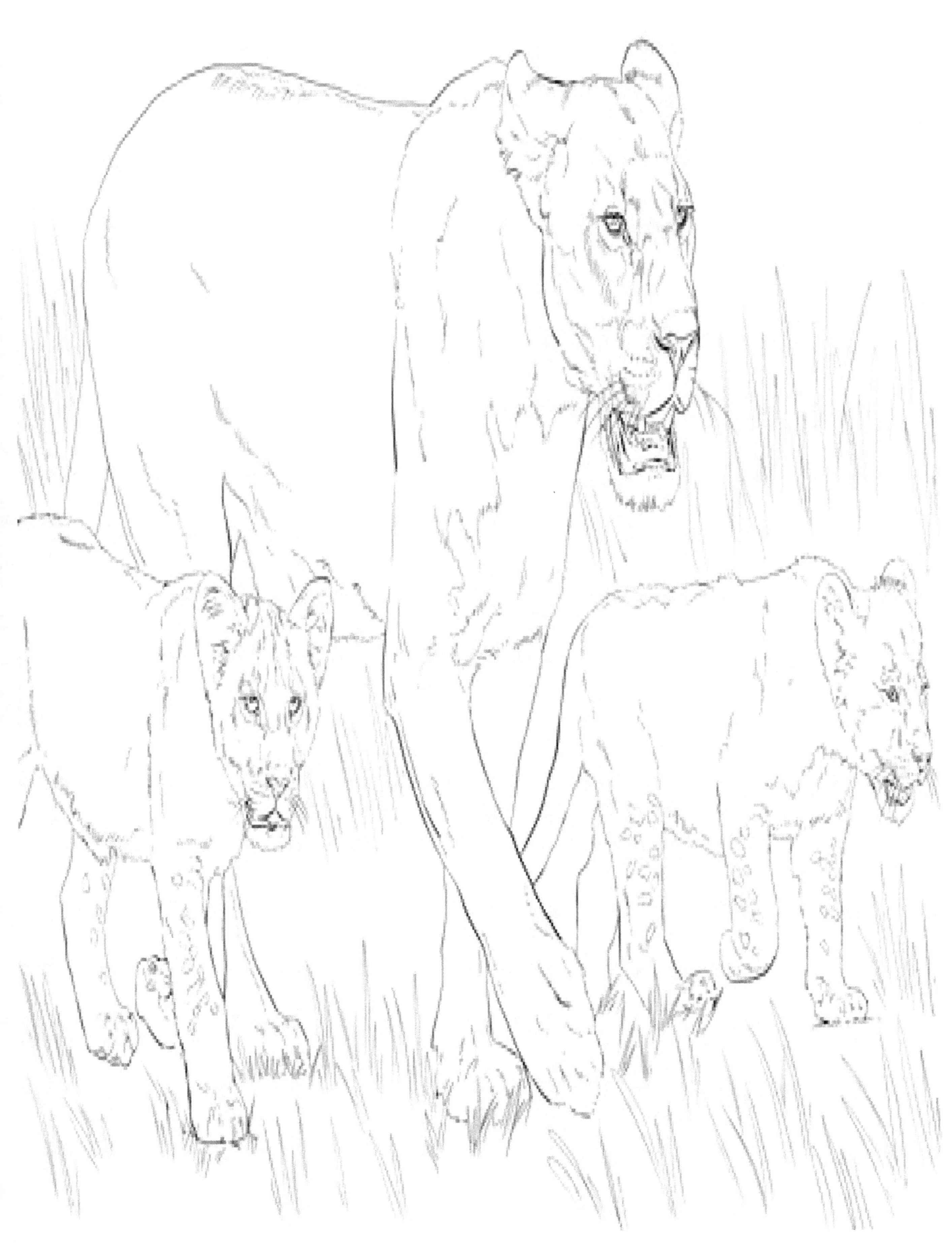

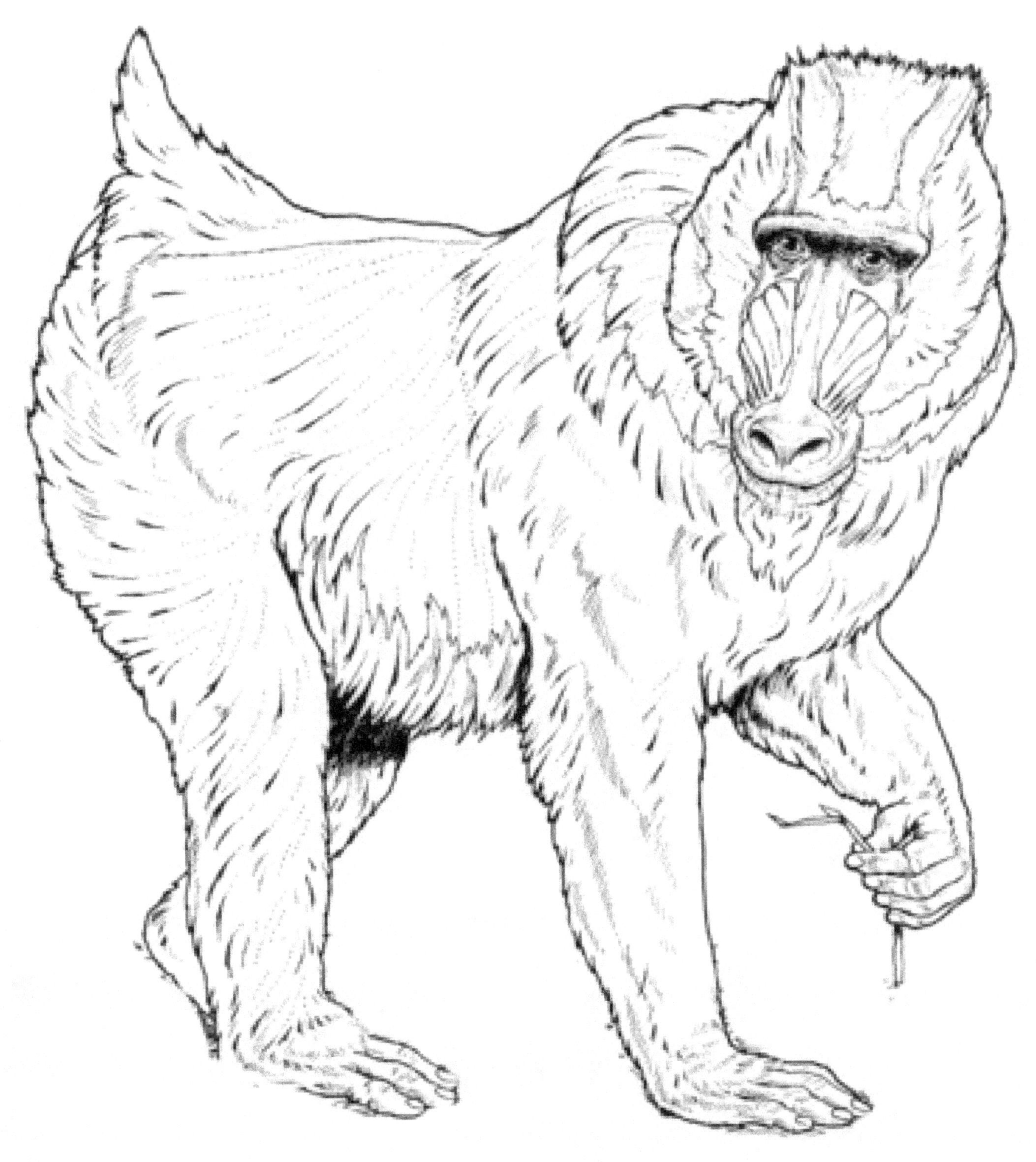

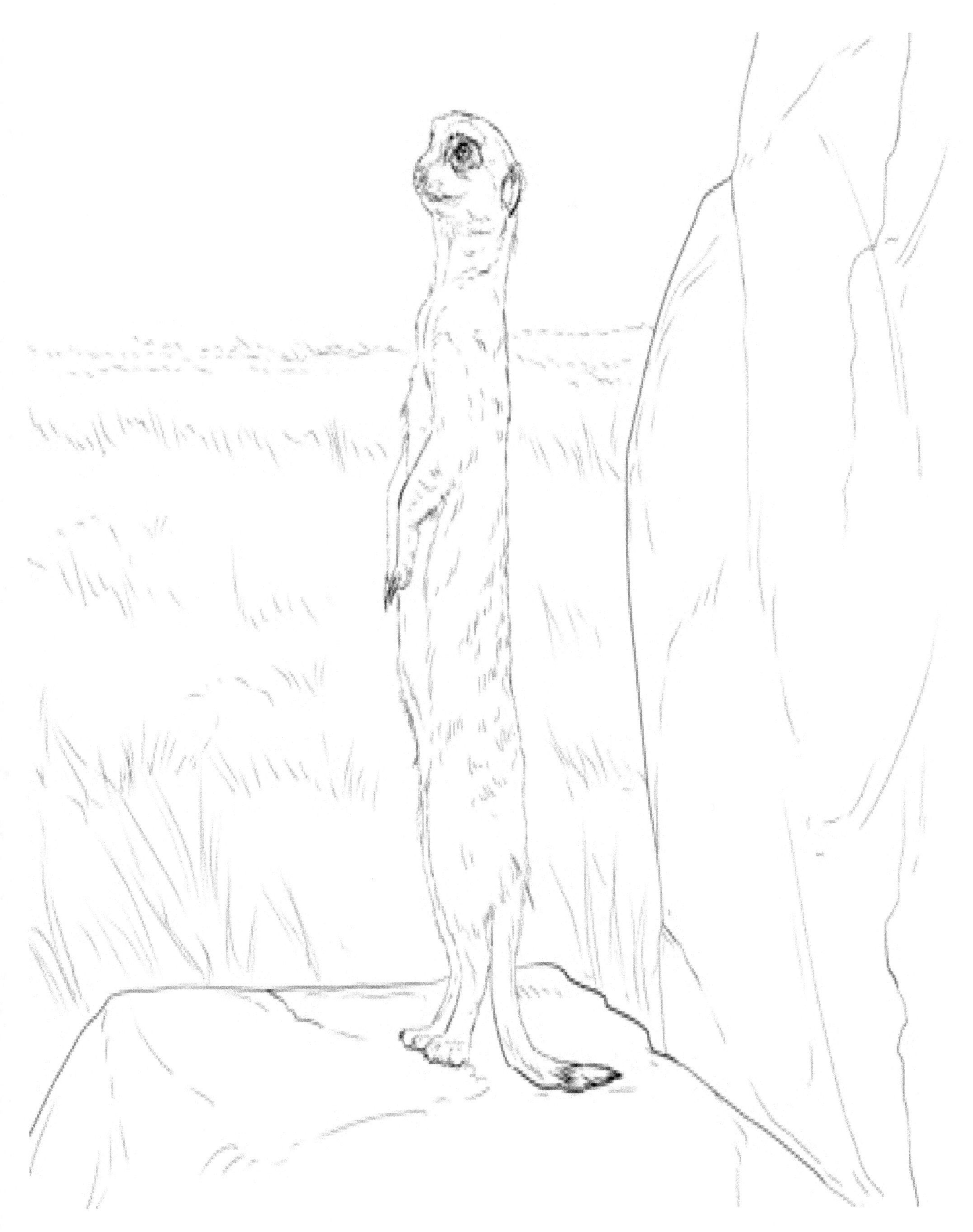

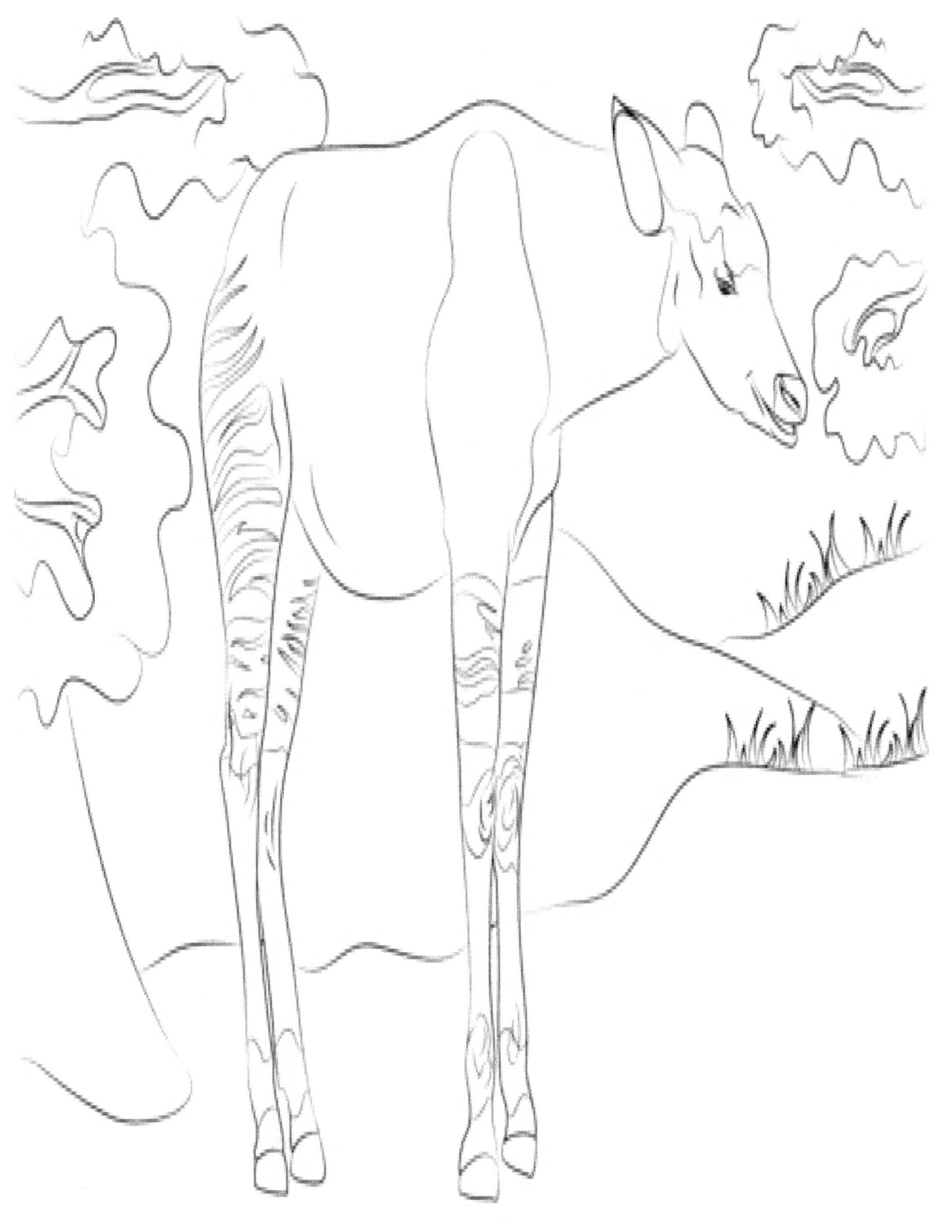

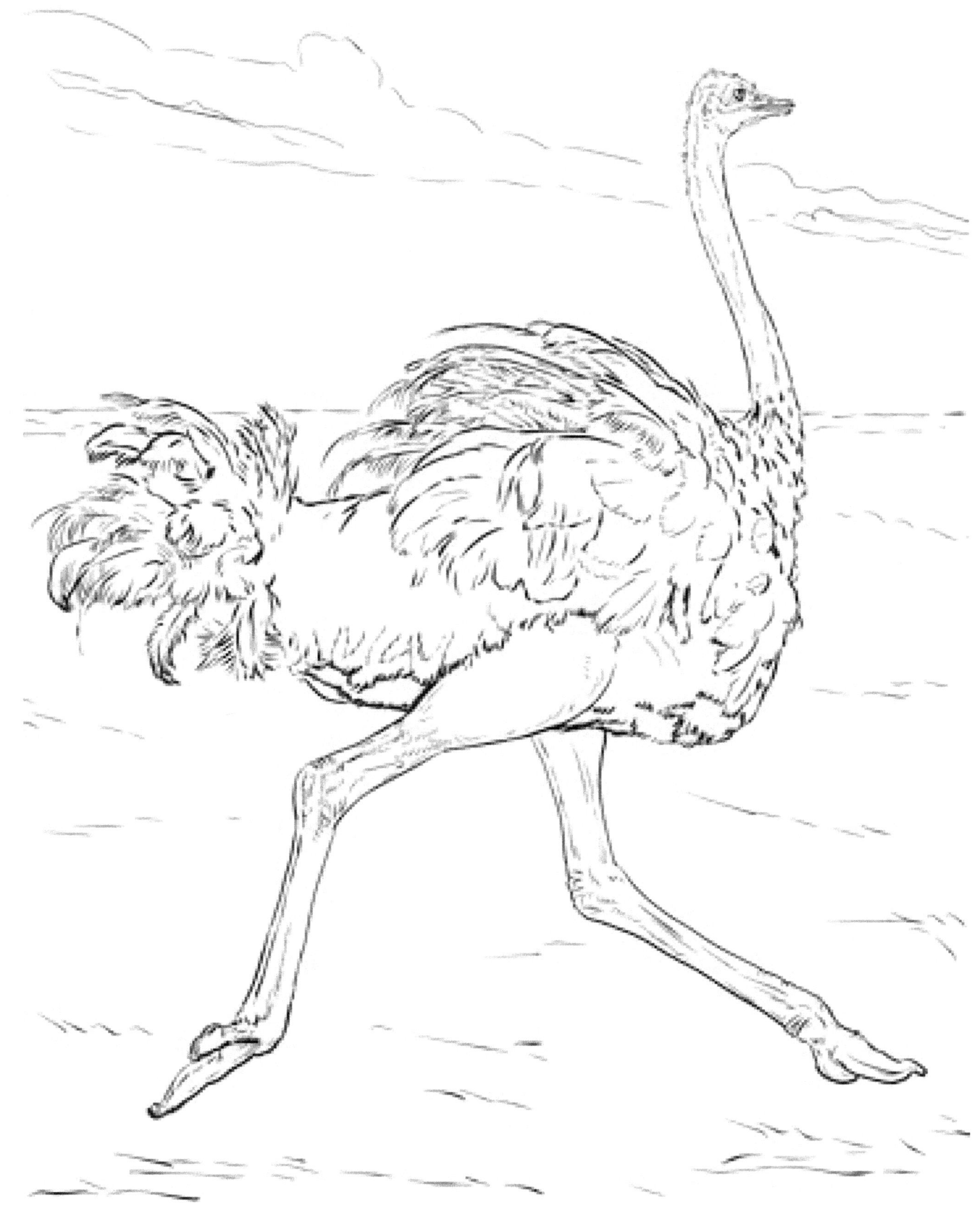

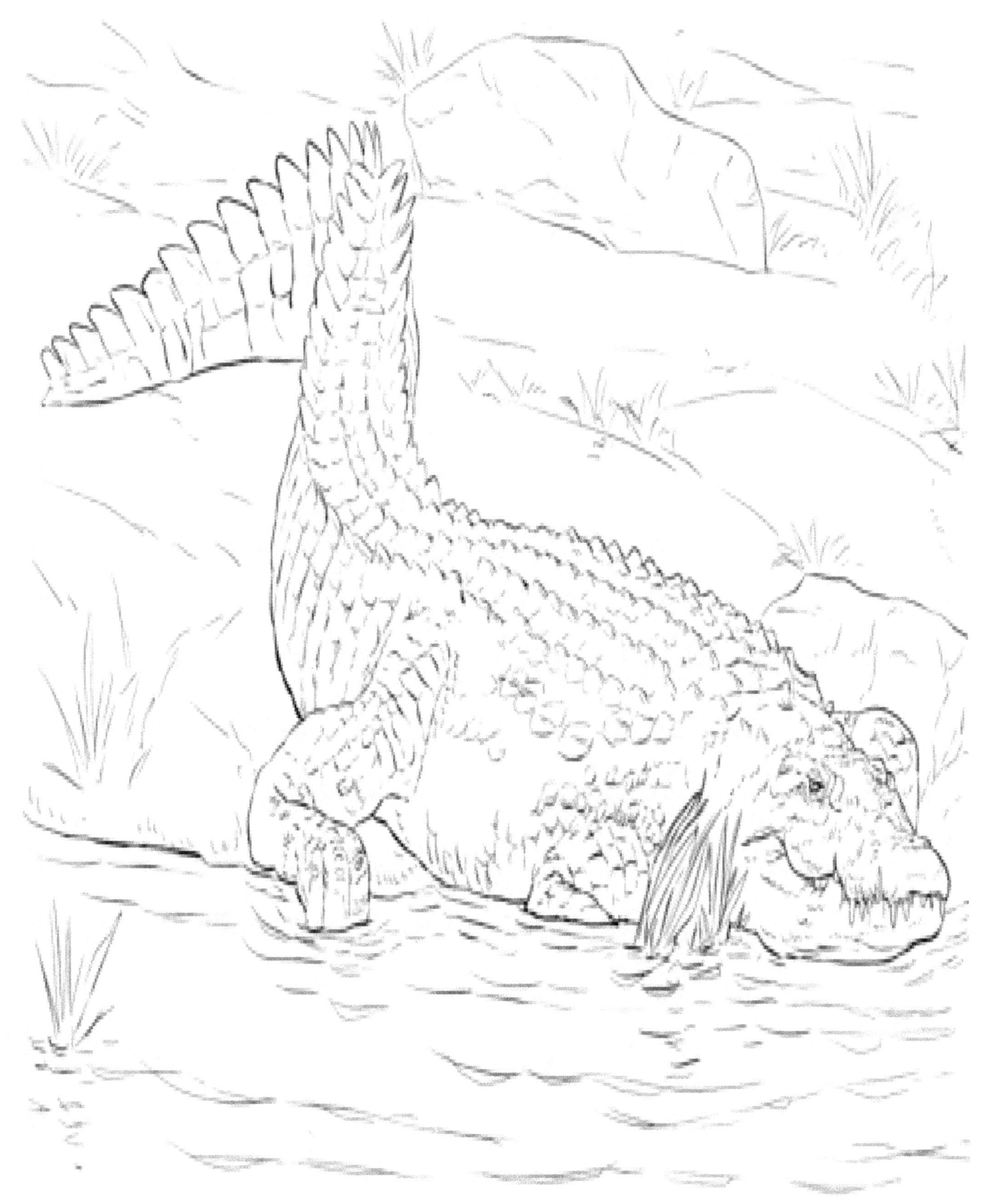

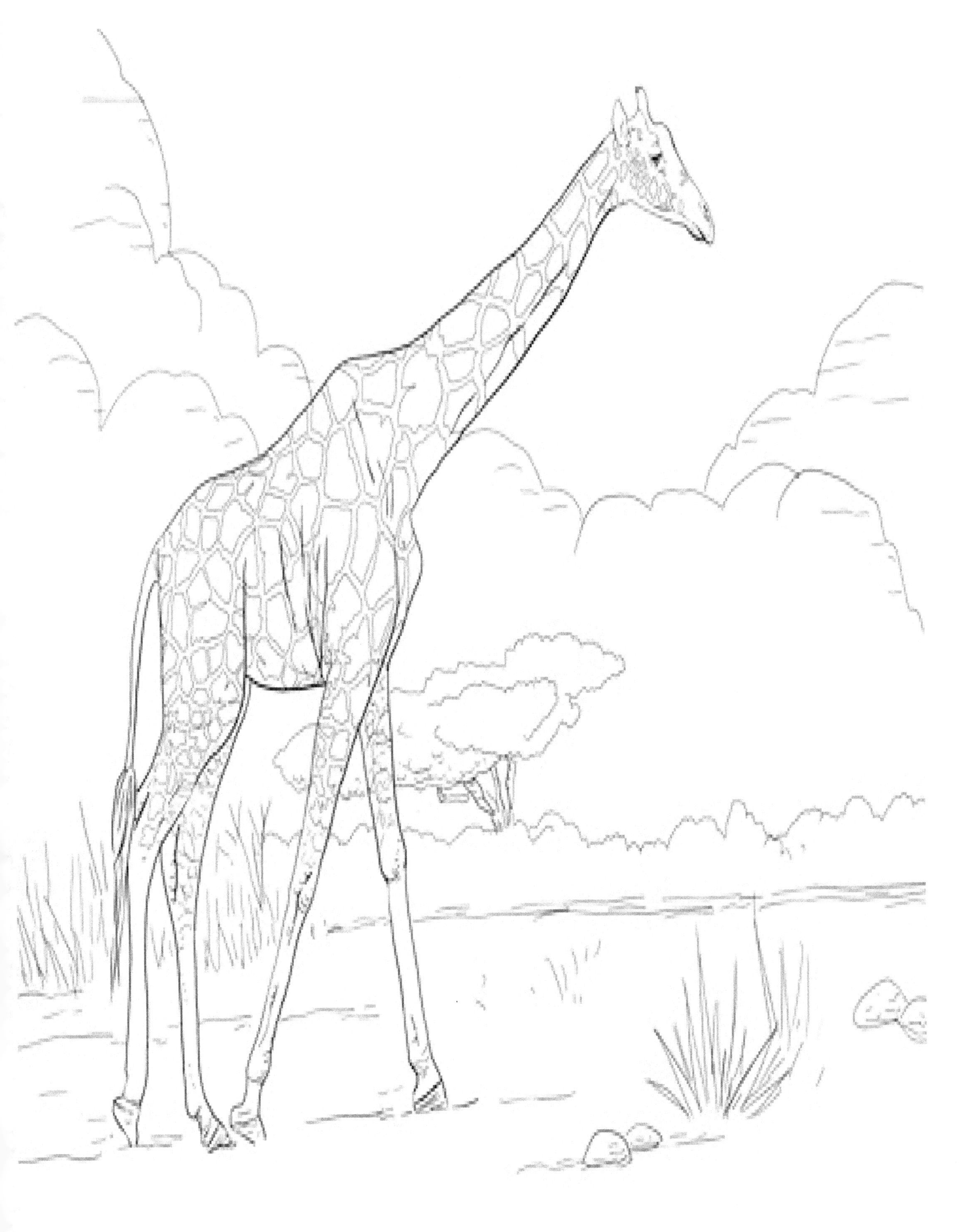

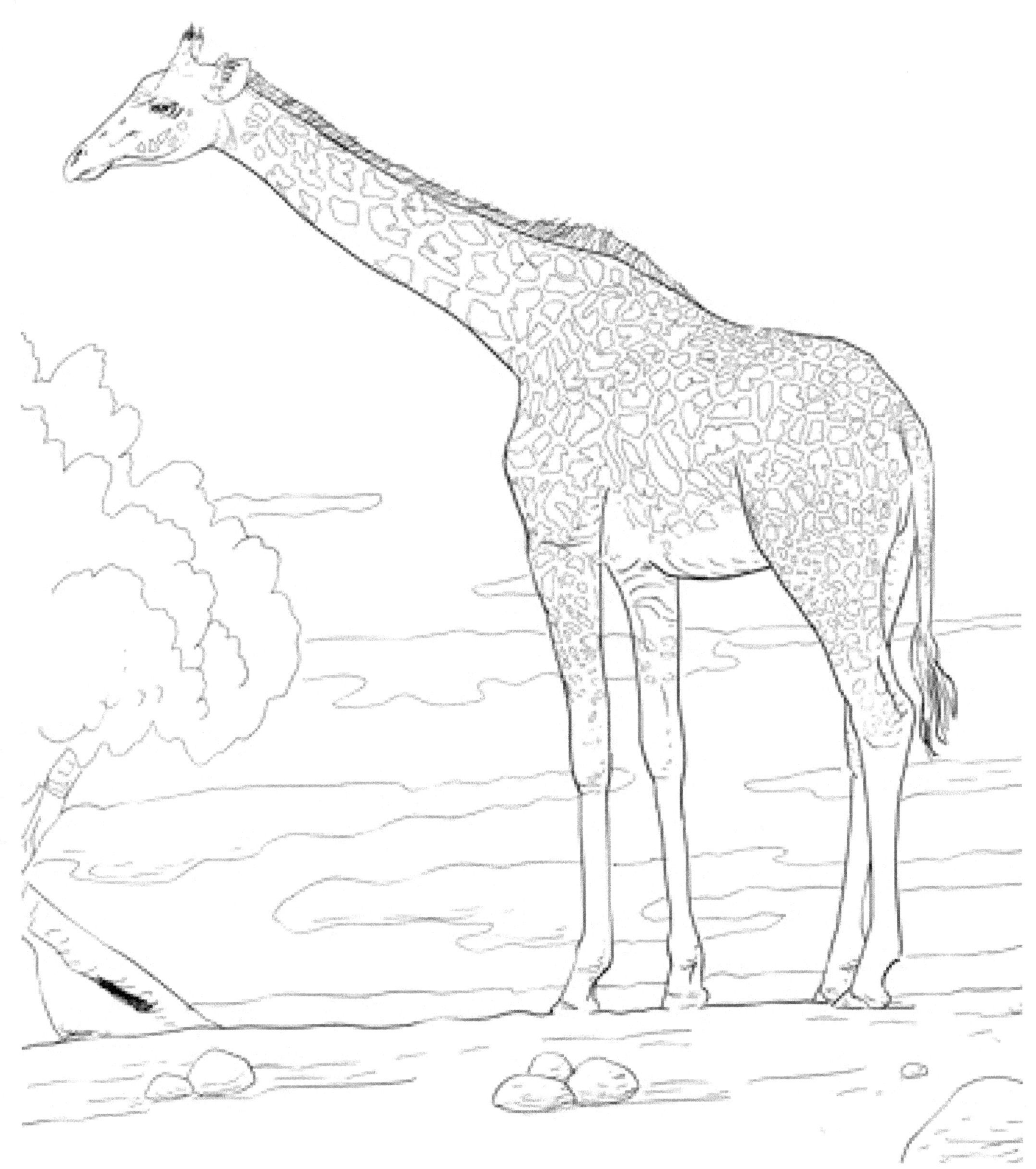

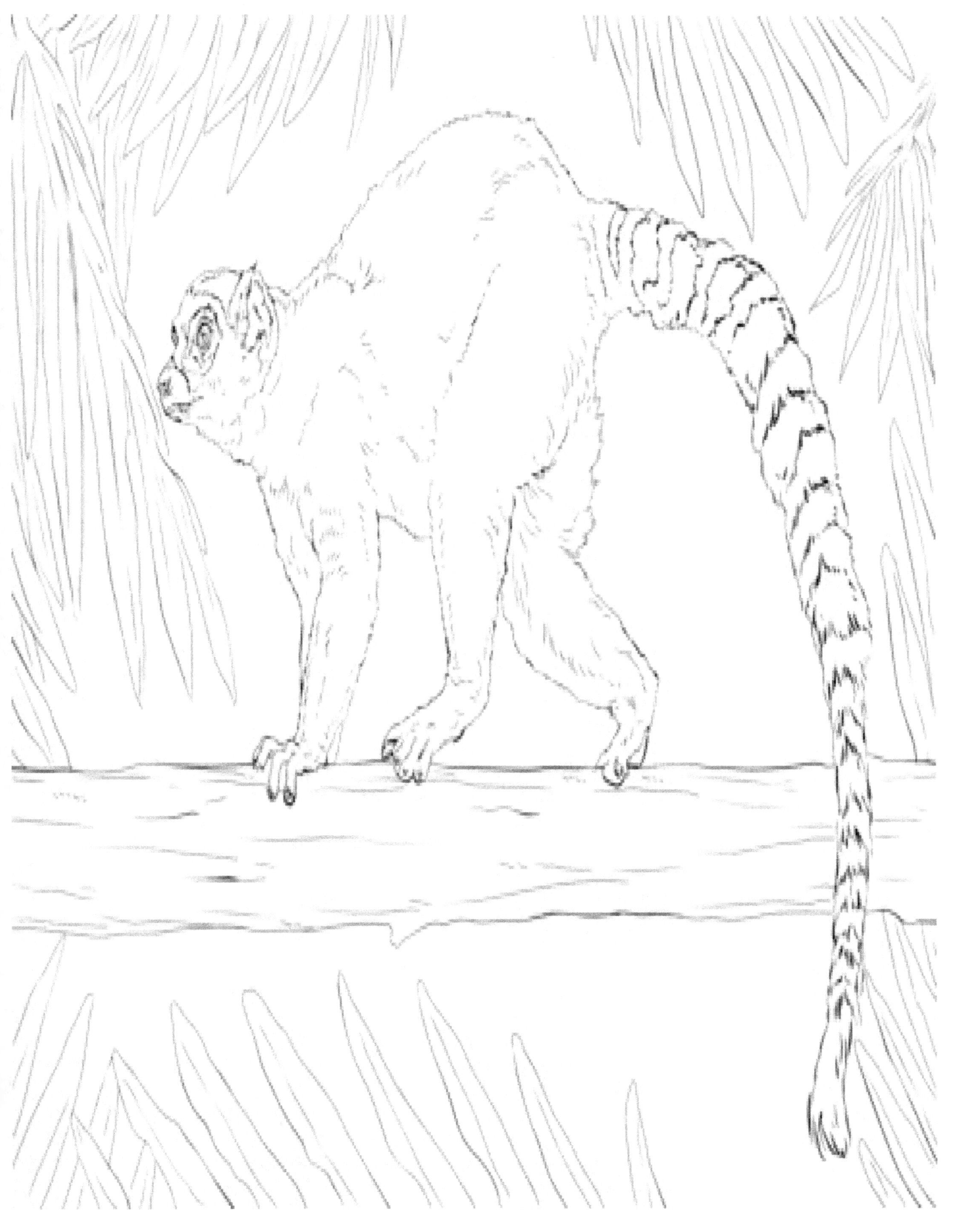

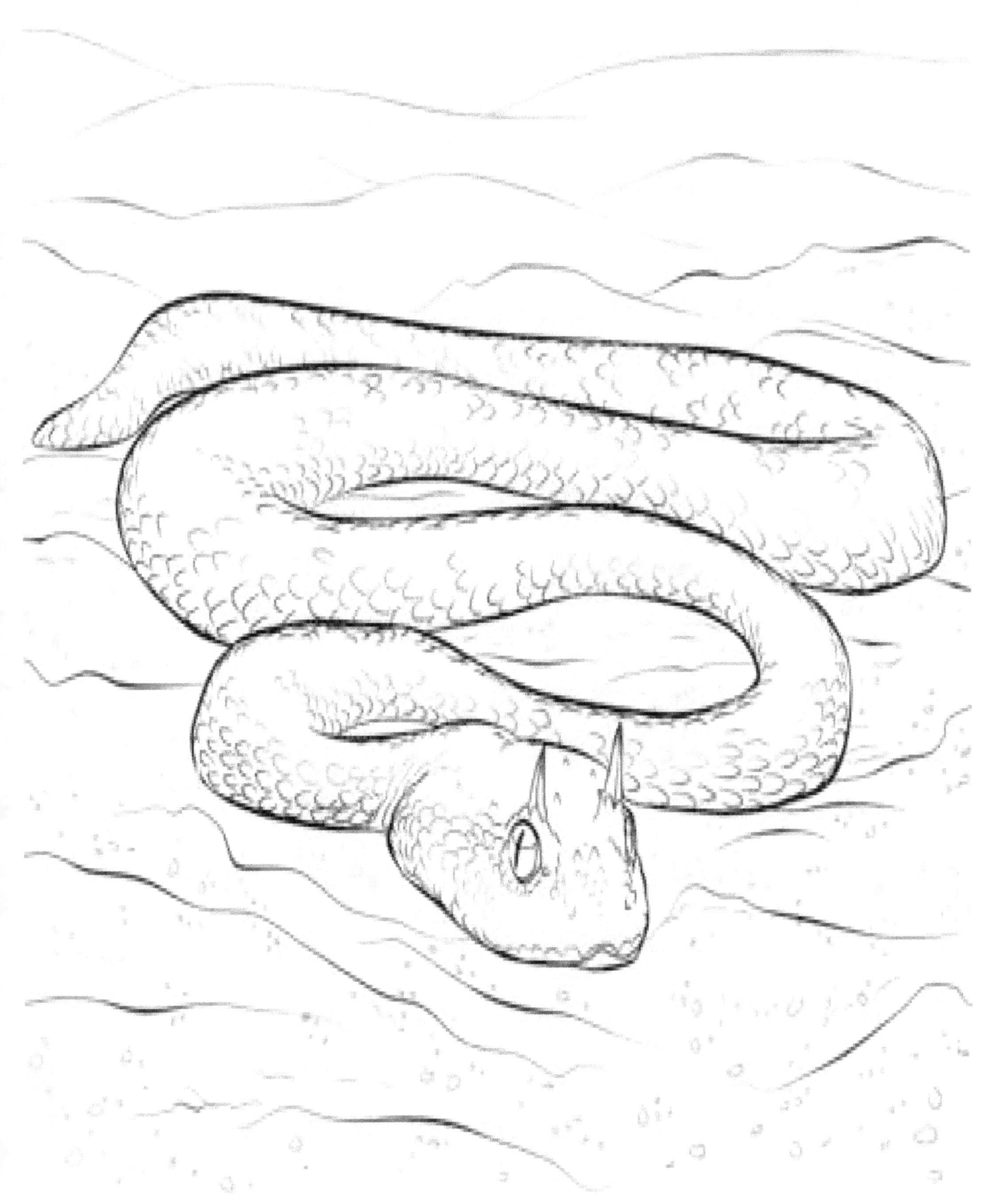

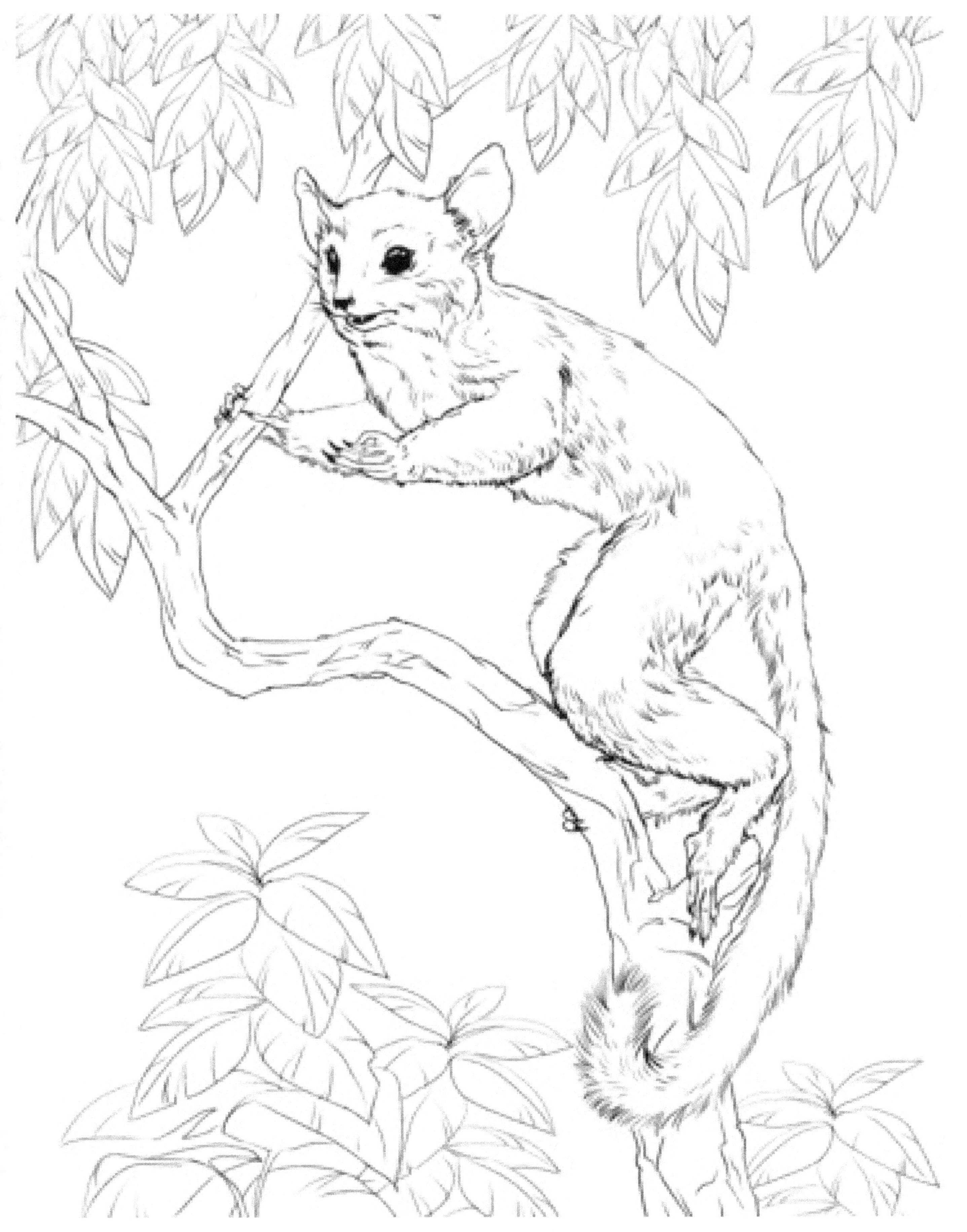

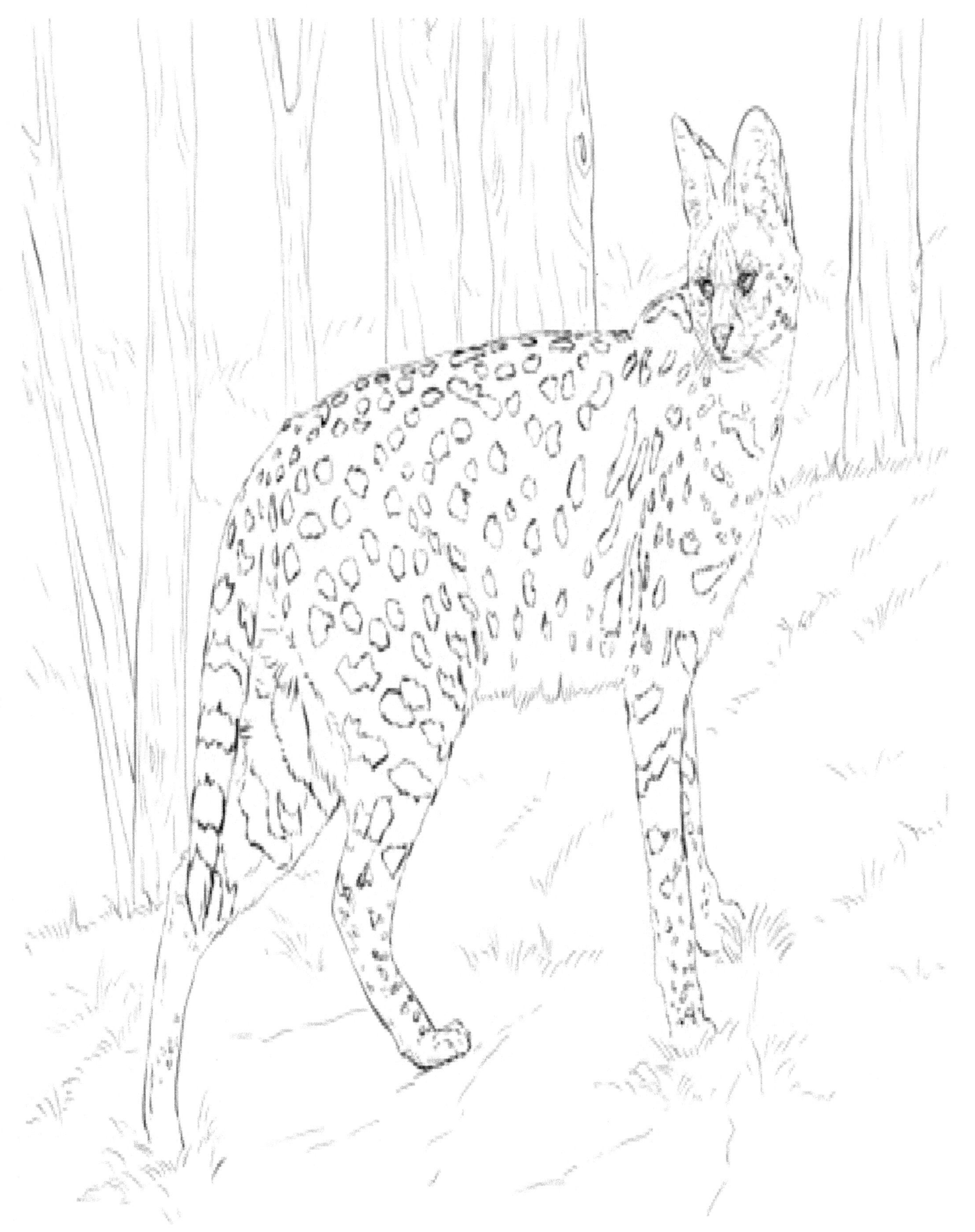

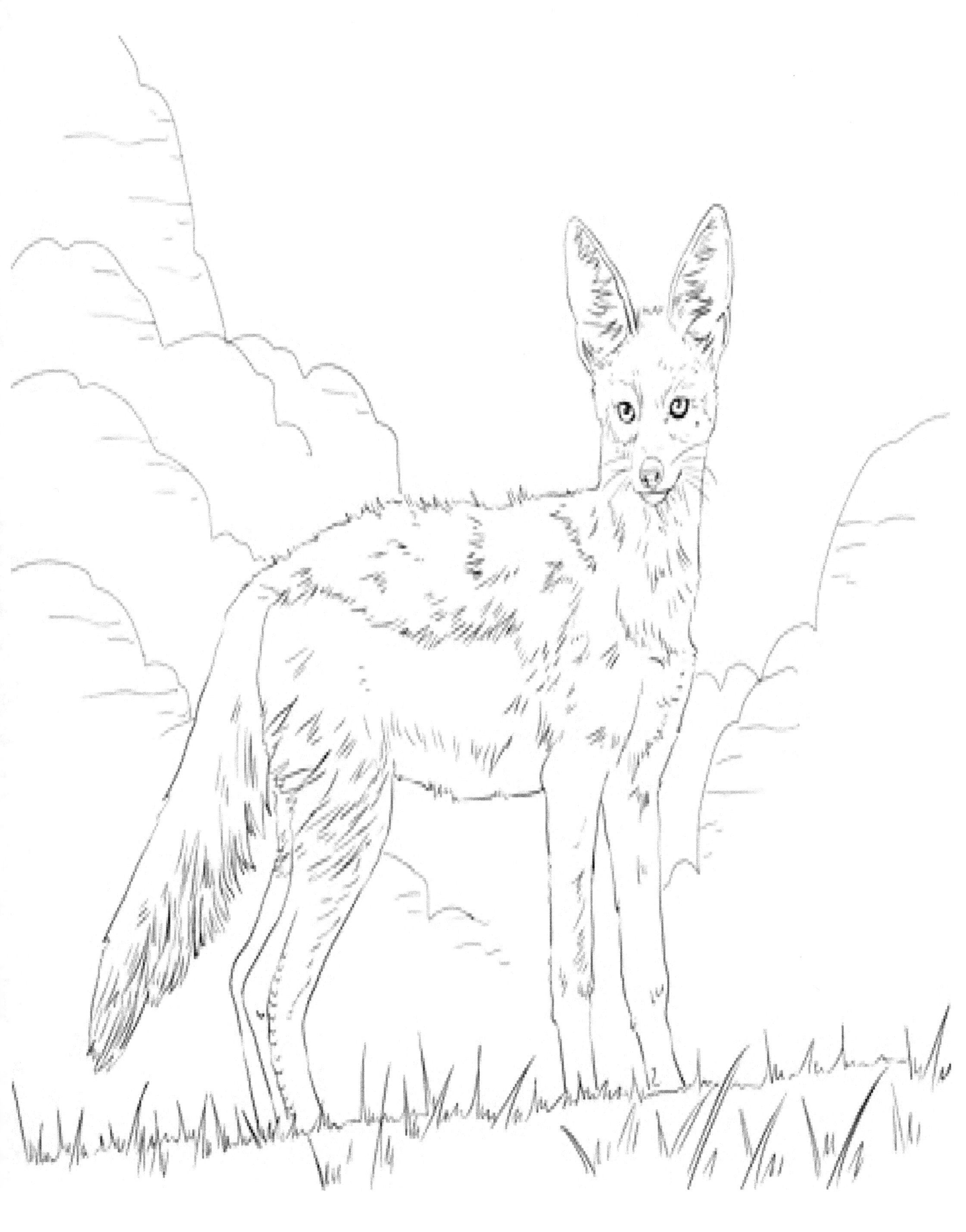

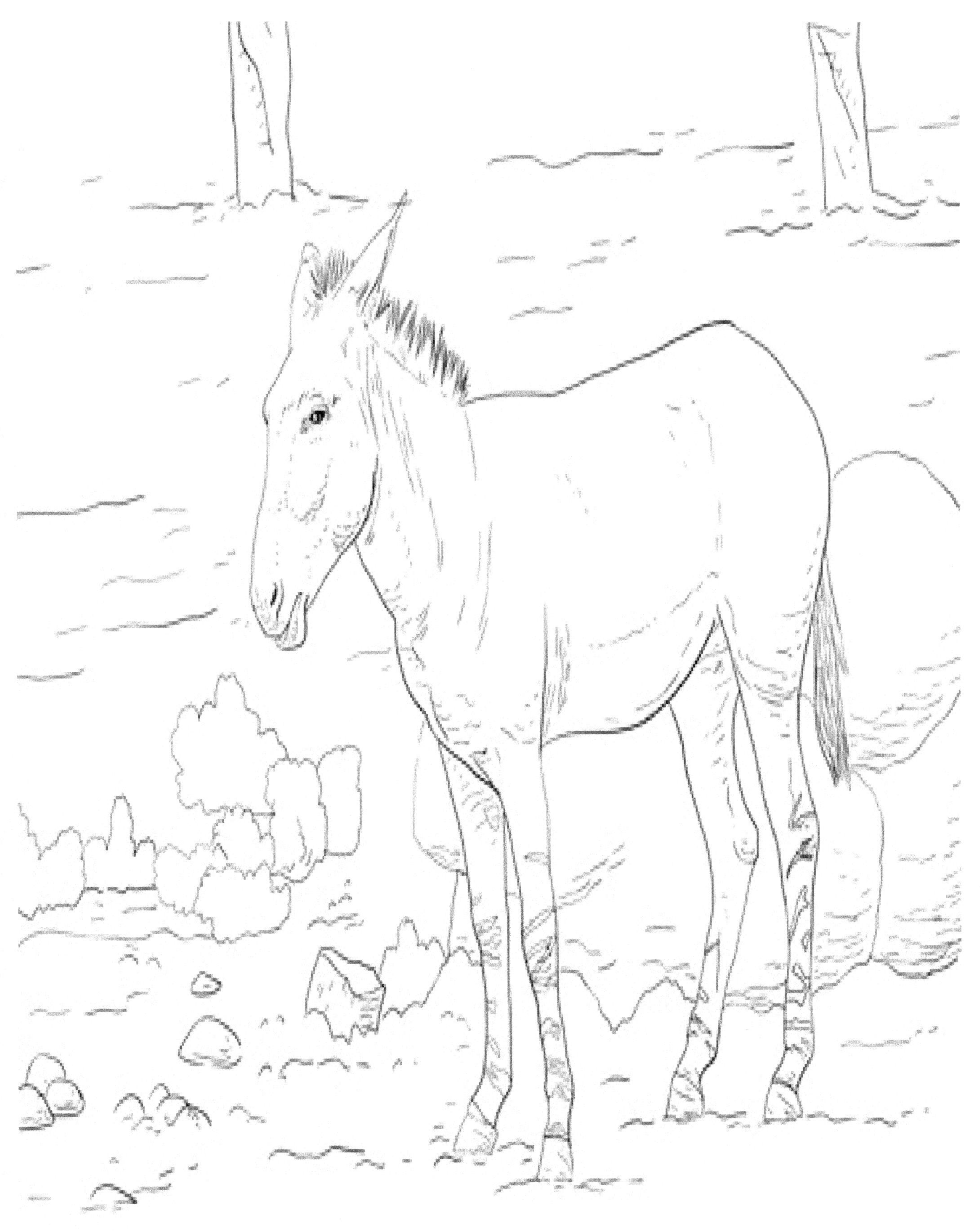

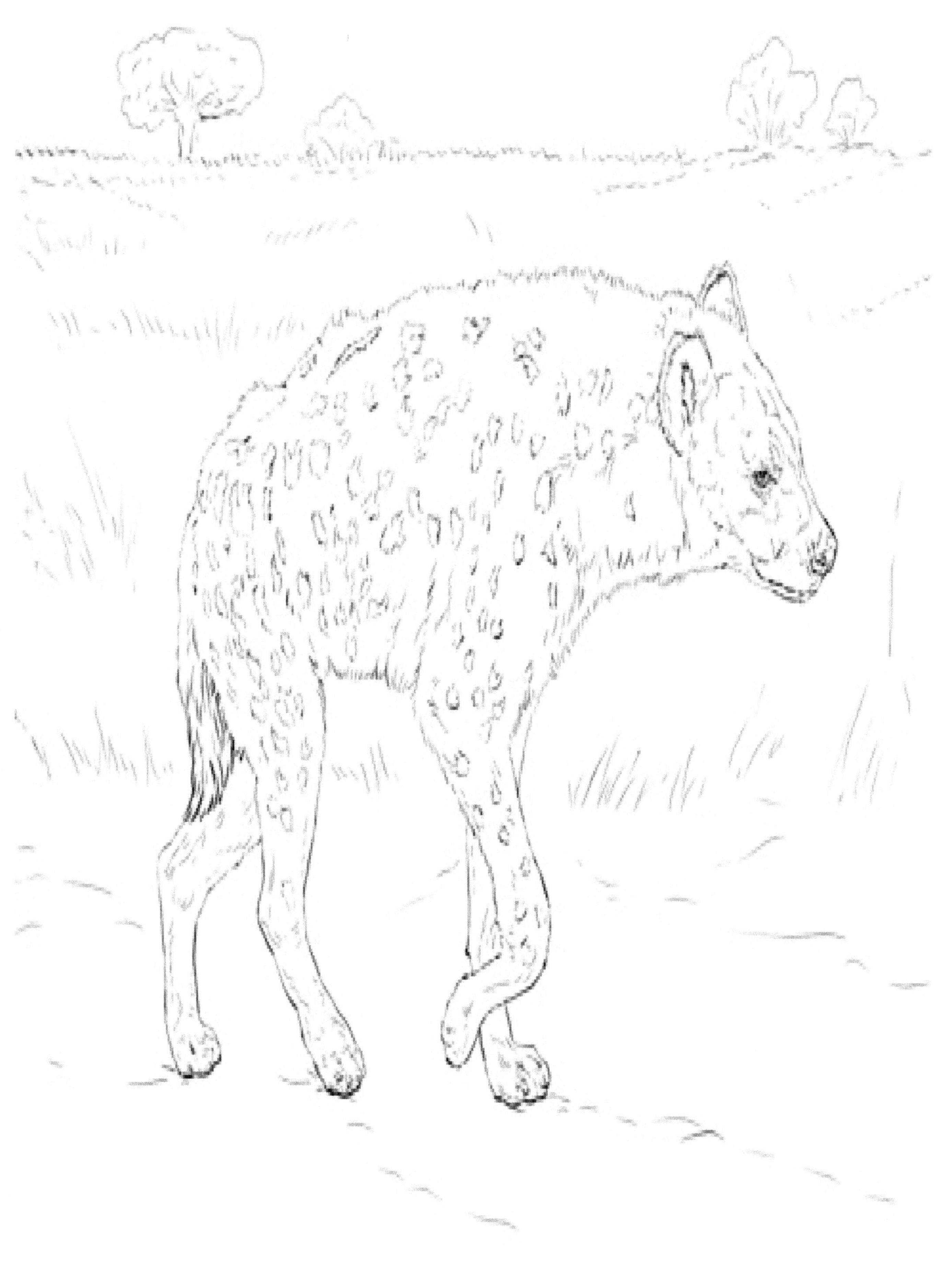

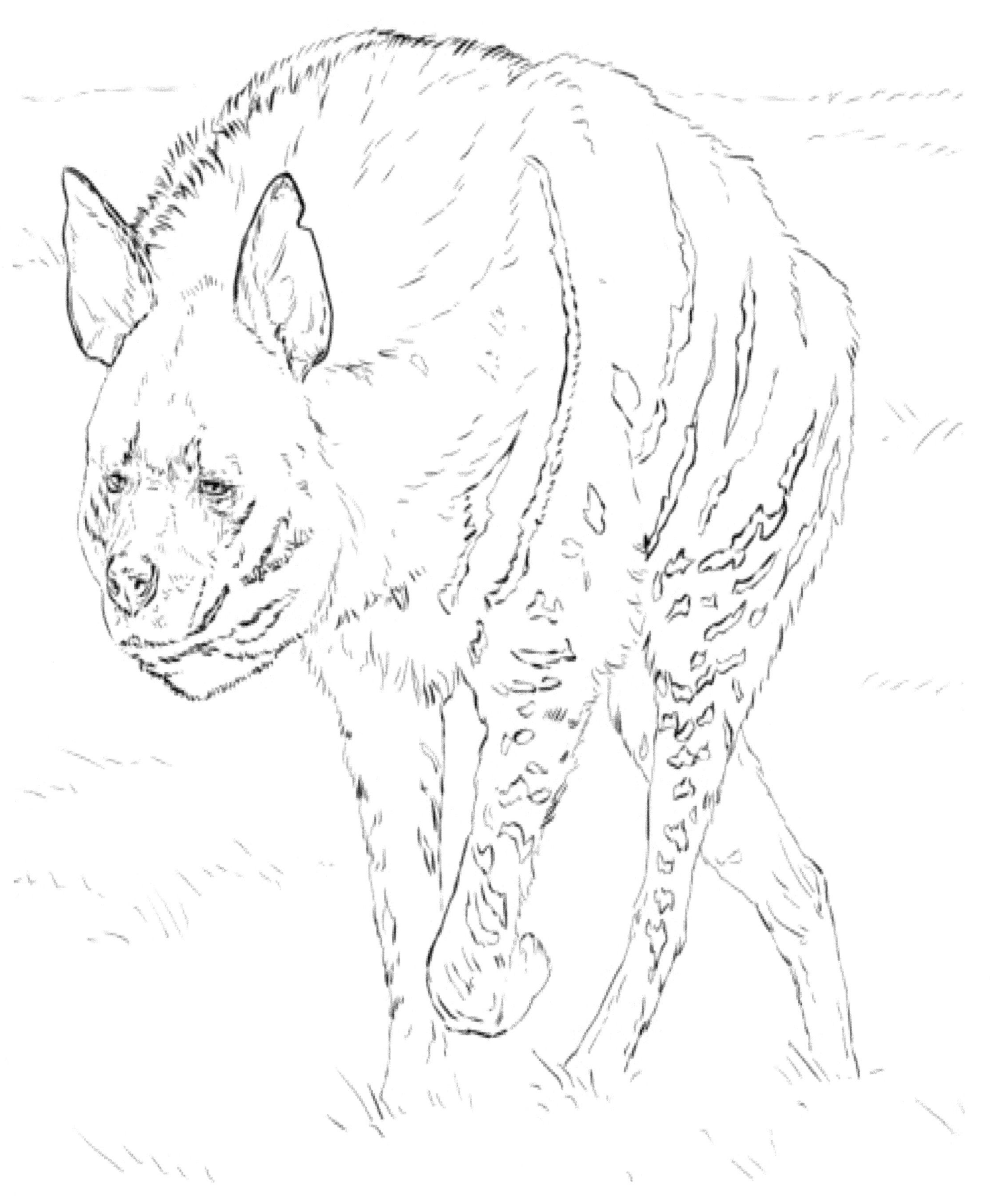

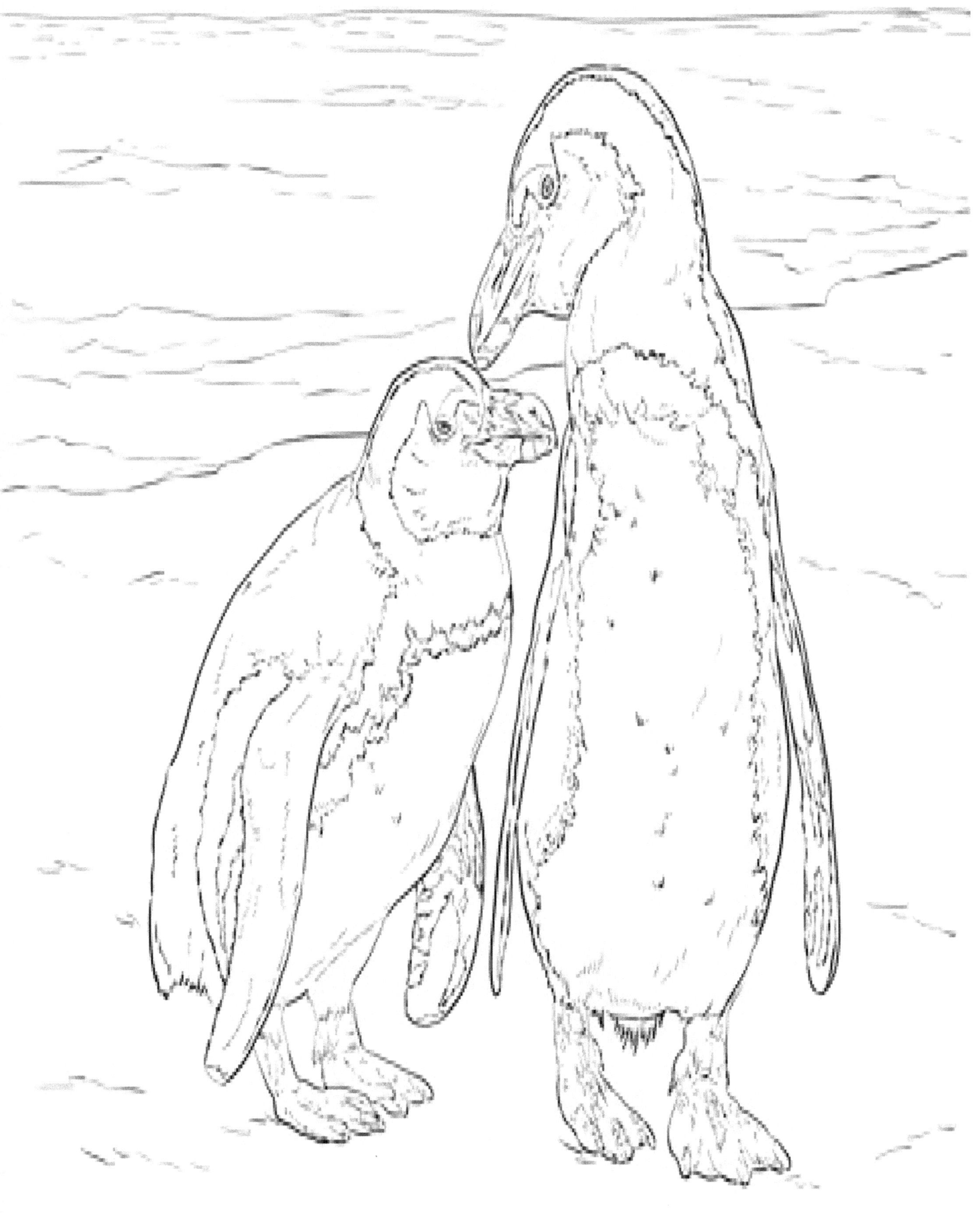

WHAT DO YOU THINK OF OUR BOOK?

We would be very grateful if you could leave us a review

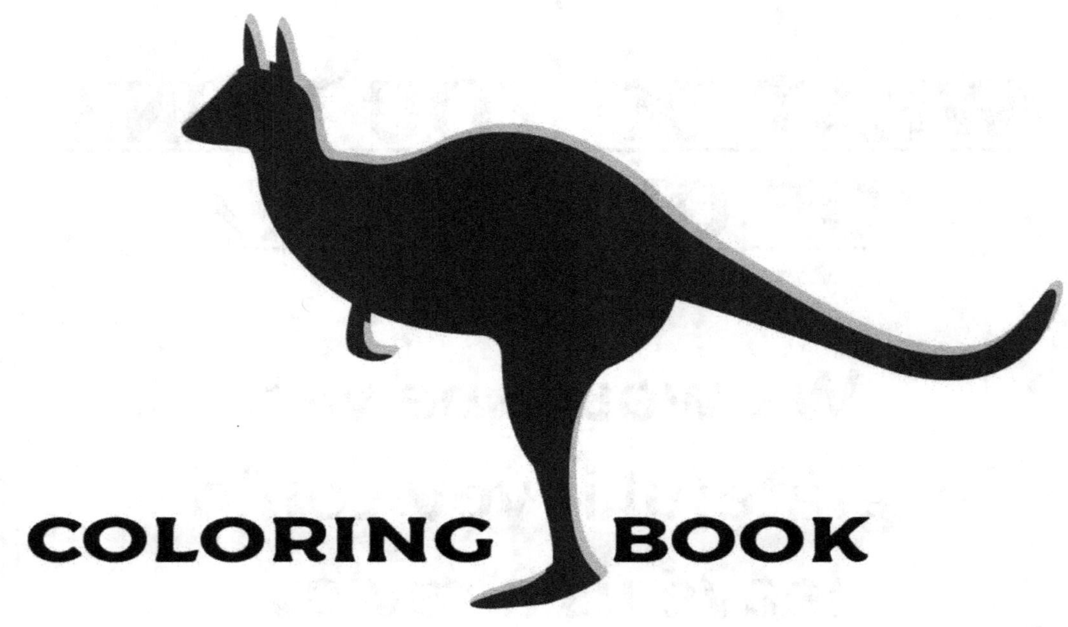
COLORING BOOK